MUSLIM AMERICAN POLITICS AND THE FUTURE OF US DEMOCRACY

Muslim American Politics and the Future of US Democracy

Edward E. Curtis IV

NEW YORK UNIVERSITY PRESS

New York

NEW YORK UNIVERSITY PRESS
New York
www.nyupress.org

References to Internet websites (URLs) were accurate at the time of writing. Neither the author nor New York University Press is responsible for URLs that may have expired or changed since the manuscript was prepared.

Library of Congress Cataloging-in-Publication Data
Names: Curtis, Edward E., 1970–   author.
Title: Muslim American politics and the future of US democracy / Edward E. Curtis IV.
Description: New York : NYU Press, 2019. | Includes bibliographical references and index.
Identifiers: LCCN 2019006868| ISBN 9781479875009 (cl : alk. paper) |
ISBN 9781479811441 (pb : alk. paper)
Subjects: LCSH: Muslims—Political activity—United States. | Islam and politics—United States. | Political participation—United States. | Political culture—United States.
Classification: LCC E184.M88 C875 2019 | DDC 297.2/72—dc23
LC record available at https://lccn.loc.gov/2019006868

New York University Press books are printed on acid-free paper, and their binding materials are chosen for strength and durability. We strive to use environmentally responsible suppliers and materials to the greatest extent possible in publishing our books.

Manufactured in the United States of America

10 9 8 7 6 5 4 3 2 1

Also available as an ebook

CONTENTS

Introduction

Once asked by a French reporter about the "Negro problem" in the United States, African American writer Richard Wright replied that "there isn't any Negro problem; there is only a white problem." Black studies scholar George Lipsitz points out that "by inverting the reporter's question, Wright called attention to its hidden assumptions—that racial polarization comes from the existence of blacks rather than the behavior of whites, that black people are a 'problem' for whites rather than fellow citizens, and that, unless otherwise specified, 'Americans' means 'whites.'"[1] Though Wright's response to anti-Black racism remains relevant primarily to the discussion of African American life, this formulation can also shed light on the way in which Muslim Americans function as a religious and often racial Other who are denied full political and social citizenship in the United States.

The future of US democracy depends on the question of whether Muslim Americans are able to exercise their political rights as US citizens and whether they can find acceptance as social equals in US society. This statement is not hyperbolic. The place of Muslims in the United States is a bellwether for the nation's purported embrace of liberal values such as freedom of speech and religion, equal justice under law, and equal opportunity. These values are the primordial symbols of liberal democracy. They are embraced by Republicans and Democrats. But these values do not apply to all Americans. They often do not apply to Muslims. The problem is not Muslims; the problem is America. Though many Muslims have sought to contribute to the democratic life of the United States since the 1950s, their efforts to "be" or "become" American have not protected their basic liberties. Even when Muslims proudly embraced assimilation, the terms under which they negotiated their political belonging to America failed them. This book explains why the nation is, at best, ambivalent about Muslim political participation and, at worst, terribly cruel. Neither the Republican nor the Democratic Party has offered full equality to Muslim Americans because these parties' politics are inextricably bound to policies and orientations that operate partly through the denial of Muslim people's full humanity and dignity.

Muslim American politics have been a barometer of US democracy since the 1950s. Though small in numbers, the presence of Muslims on American soil rose to national political prominence during the Cold War and then the twenty-first-century war on terror. They have often acted as the social and political margin against which the center of US political belonging has been forged. In the 1950s and 1960s, it was the Nation of Islam, at the time the largest and best-known US Muslim group, and Malcolm X that played a foil in political debates over civil rights and US foreign policy. Defined by Republicans and Democrats alike as a religious cult and a radical political threat to the republic, the Nation of Islam was constructed by liberal civil rights icons such as Thurgood Marshall as a form of Black nationalism that must be rejected and even surveilled by the government. Likewise, Malcolm X's emerging Islamic ethics of revolution was seen as a threat to America not only because Malcolm X reminded Black people of their (liberal) rights to self-defense but also because he organized opposition to US neocolonial control and military intervention in the Global South. During the Cold War, Black Muslims linked the domestic challenge of anti-Black racism to the struggle for Afro-Asian self-determination. Their repression by the federal government exposed the extent to which American democracy was not only hypocritical, but also fundamentally undemocratic in its racist and imperial orientation.

Similarly, in the era after the attacks of September 11, 2001, so-called immigrant Muslims—some of whom could trace their family histories in the United States to the late 1800s and early 1900s—became a fundamental "problem" for US democracy. The central role of Muslims in American political life was made plain when, after Donald Trump's election in 2016, foreign visitors from several Muslim-majority countries were banned from entering the United States. But even before President Trump made a home in the Oval Office for blatantly racist anti-Muslim rhetoric, the administrations of both George W. Bush and Barack Obama showed how American political values such as religious liberty, freedom from unreasonable searches, and guarantees of equal protection under the law were too often null and void when it came to both Muslim American citizens and Muslims living under US military occupation or political control. Since 9/11, the treatment of Muslims has exposed the rotten core of American democracy, and that rot has been disturbingly bipartisan.

The main argument of the book is that dominant forms of American liberalism have prevented the political assimilation of Muslim Americans; Muslim Americans have sometimes resisted and more frequently accommodated American liberalism, but in either case, they have never been afforded full citizenship. In scrutinizing the role of liberalism in preventing the assimilation of Muslims into the nation-state, I focus on liberalism as an institutionalized, structural reality that assumes power in a variety of social, economic, and political domains, especially in the military, foreign policy, the courts, and law enforcement agencies.[2] I contend (1) that racism and imperialism have been central to the practice of American liberalism; (2) that Muslims have played especially prominent roles since the 1950s in the way that American liberalism has unfolded; and (3) that Muslims have both challenged and sustained a form of liberalism that offers them only limited inclusion in the republic.

Liberalism is a much disputed and debated ideology whose meaning has changed over time, but one of its core elements in the context of US politics is the idea that the government has the responsibility to protect and advance the liberty of individuals. The American Declaration of Independence and the US Constitution's Bill of Rights identify human individuals—and their rights to property, free speech, the free exercise of religion, and so on—as the foundation of a just, functioning nation. But not everyone in the American nation-state has been considered worthy of liberty. As it was institutionalized and practiced in the United States, liberalism excluded Native Americans, Africans, women, and others. The franchise was given mainly to white men, who ruled an ethno-national state. American freedom and democracy for white men rested on the ethnic cleansing of Native Americans—who were not considered part of "the people"—and on the racialization of human slavery. The nation not only denied liberty to racial others, it also made and enforced laws designed to protect the people—that is, the dominant ethno-racial group—from the aliens in their midst. Thus, the freedom of white people was created through the denial of liberty to African Americans and other nonwhites who lived under colonial domination inside their own country.[3]

From the earliest days of the republic, the racist logic of American liberalism extended to its war-making abroad. As it so happened, the American form of liberalism was also defined in opposition to Islamic religion and Muslim cultures. The first overseas war conducted by the United States was fought from 1801 to 1805 against the North African principality of Tripoli, which demanded tribute from US-flagged ships that wished to pass safely through its waters. American leaders insisted that these levies were a form of bondage that threatened freedom of movement and trade. The federal government did not pay up, and after American ships were detained by the so-called Barbary states, Thomas Jefferson's 1800 presidential campaign criticized the nation's second president, John Adams, who preferred to negotiate his way out of the impasse. The newly elected Jefferson decided instead to go to war. The US Navy largely dominated the seas during the conflict, but when sailors of the *U.S.S. Philadelphia* were taken prisoner in 1803, the tough-talking Jefferson reversed course and ended up negotiating a truce with their captors in exchange for $60,000 in ransom.[4] From that time until the present, war-making in Muslim lands has been frequently interpreted by US policymakers and citizens alike as a struggle for liberty and freedom over and against what are said, in blatantly racist terms, to be Islam's and Muslims' tendencies toward despotism, ignorance, and fanaticism.[5] As

we will see in the chapters that follow, US liberalism's supposedly benevolent military intervention abroad, including in places where Muslims
live, is essential to explaining why Muslim Americans are not offered full
political and social citizenship in the United States.

American liberals have imagined the United States as an exceptional
nation, often as a divinely ordained "city on a hill" with a solemn duty
to liberate the earth from those who would prevent the free exchange of
ideas and goods. In this mythological view of America, it is America's
calling to protect and serve the ideals of individual liberty at any cost.[6]
As this ideology of American global leadership took root and assumed
form, US political leaders explained why it was necessary and often ben-
eficial to occupy the lands of Native Americans and later to colonize Ha-
waii, Guam, Puerto Rico, and the Philippines, where the United States
occupied and eventually massacred an indigenous Muslim population
during battles at Bud Dajo and Bud Bagsak.[7] No matter how violent it
was, the American empire was framed as consonant with liberal ideals, a
benevolent intervention essential to the global expansion of democracy,
free markets, and individual rights.[8]

For much of US history, the practice of an ethno-racial, colonial liberalism caused little concern for its rulers. There were always excep-
tions, of course. But even when US political leaders sought to expand
some individual rights to nonwhite people, they often did so in a way
that preserved white supremacy in either law or fact. The period after
World War II was different, however, as a critical mass of US politicians
began to pass laws designed to ensure that liberalism's promise applied
to people of color as well as to whites, to women as well as to men, to
immigrants as well as to native-born Americans. It is important to note
that both Democrats and Republicans in this era were proponents of
liberalism—notwithstanding the popular understanding that a "liberal"
is the same as a Democrat. Democrats and Republicans debated which
laws and policies would best protect and promote individual liberty and
the pursuit of happiness, but they were largely united in their devotion
to liberalism in contradistinction to socialism and communism. Insti-

tutional liberalism became associated in the 1950s with so-called consensus politics, defined not only by opposition to the Soviet Union and
communism but also by its support of a variety of sometimes contradictory elements. Postwar institutional liberalism largely supported the
welfare state, corporate rights, the repression of domestic dissent, and
the expansion of individual religious liberty along with a theoretical sep-
aration of religion from the state. As many proponents of liberalism are
inclined to point out, squashing domestic dissent is something liberals
should oppose. But the experience of Muslim Americans demonstrates
the necessity of describing liberalism as it actually was and is, liberalism
in practice, not liberalism in theory—that is, what its proponents wished
it could be. The denial of freedom to Black people, for example, has been
perfectly compatible with the lived reality of institutional liberalism.[9]
And as Africana religions scholar Sylvester Johnson points out, "the relationship between freedom and its others has to be *explained* instead
of being dismissed as mere hypocrisy or contradiction."[10] To do so in
the United States, one has to explain the denial of freedom to Muslim
Americans since World War II.

Muslim Americans have long hoped that they might become full
citizens in the United States, and American political leaders have offered rhetorical support for their assimilation. Beginning with President Eisenhower and continuing through President Obama, both
Republican and Democratic presidents have articulated the idea that
Muslims, like other religious minorities, can become genuine Americans, especially if they willing to serve in the US military and fight its
ideological enemies. They, too, could enjoy the fruits of liberalism. But
at the same time that these presidents called out Muslims as potential
citizens deserving of American rights and liberties, their policies and
rhetoric alienated Muslims from the liberal dream. Because American
liberalism in practice accommodated racism at home and colonial intervention in the developing world, the state often framed anyone who
opposed the status quo, including white supremacy and military domination abroad, as a potential enemy.

This is why politics rather than culture is key to understanding the assimilation of Muslim Americans. There is a popular, liberal idea that over time Muslim Americans will be accepted like every other immigrant group—it is said that as Muslims assimilate to US culture, US culture will be able to assimilate them. But any theory that explains contemporary anti-Muslim bias, discrimination, and violence in terms of cultural difference rather than the dynamics of US politics naively or perhaps cynically ignores the roots of the American problem with Muslims. Some of the fiercest Muslim American critics of US democracy have been African Americans, who are not only assimilated to US culture but who have played an inordinately large role in creating it from the 1600s until today. This is why African American Muslims have been able to mount effective criticism of the United States—put bluntly, Black people know America and how America works. Blaming cultural difference for a lack of assimilation may not be sound analysis but it can be an effective rhetorical strategy, as Richard Wright pointed out, to blame the victims of US democracy for their lack of assimilation. As Ibram Kendi contends, some Americans have long explained anti-Black racism as a white reaction to the supposed problems of Black culture, it pathology, and its criminality.[11] Antiracist scholars have offered a more convincing case: the lack of racial equality in the United States is not the result of African American culture but instead of structural and institutional anti-Black racism.[12] When applied to the case of Muslim Americans, this approach to understanding inequality suggests that it would be fruitful to focus less on how Muslims are culturally different and more on how various cultural differences are deployed in public discourses regarding Muslim American political and social engagement.

As we will see, some of the loudest Muslim critics of American liberalism could be found in Elijah Muhammad's Nation of Islam, the most prominent Muslim organization in the United States during the 1950s and 1960s. The Nation of Islam challenged white supremacy, rejected US war-making in the developing world, criticized American nationalism, and scoffed at the allure of half-hearted, legally oriented approaches to civil rights. But it also supported various socially conservative cultural practices associated with American liberalism, appealing to a politics of middle-class respectability that preached the salvific potential of heterosexuality, patriarchy, higher education, a healthy diet, modesty, punctuality, hard work, and Black capitalism. Because it was a charismatic religious movement—what was and is referred to pejoratively as a "cult"—the Nation of Islam seemed dangerous to the federal government and Black liberals alike. Even its middle-class respectability was viewed as potentially seditious because the ethics and rituals so familiar to American Protestant Christians had been reinterpreted as responses to the divine commandments of a self-styled Muslim prophet.

Still, the symbolic opposition of the Nation of Islam to white supremacy and US empire operated within the theoretically protected, if not actually observed, legal limits of dissent because it was categorized as religion. But when the movement's popular leader, Malcolm X, broke away from Elijah Muhammad in 1964 and began to articulate and organize around a more explicitly political platform that would unite people of color and Muslims across the world to oppose white supremacy and colonialism both at home and abroad, he issued a more unambiguous challenge to the liberal order. Malcolm X's theorizing and organizing, which sought both Pan-African and pan-Muslim unity, was a radical repudiation of the US-dominated "free world," which relied on a doctrine of American military superiority and direct or indirect control of African, Asian, and Latin American nation-states. Chapter 3 shows how Malik El-Shabazz, as Malcolm X would become known, developed an Islamic liberation ethics that strategically negotiated the warring interests of the Arab Cold War to gain the support of both Egypt and Saudi Arabia for the political and cultural liberation of all people of color around the world. Though he cultivated ties with Saudi Arabia, an oil-rich state considered essential to US national security interests from the postwar era until today, he also attacked the US-led liberal order that attempted to protect Middle East monarchies from the challenge of revolutionary republics and especially the Islamic socialism of Egyptian president Gamal Abdel Nasser.

Malik El-Shabazz's political radicalism is essential to understanding Muslim American politics today because he made clear the stakes of cooperating with a racist and colonial regime. Shabazz lampooned liberal African American civil rights leaders as "Uncle Toms." As long as people of color cooperated with a system that rested on US imperial domination, he argued, they would never be free or equal in the United States. At the same time, even Malcolm X's radical politics sometimes appealed to liberal ideas and liberal institutions, especially the United Nations, as he sought to advance his political agenda of Black liberation.

The postwar US political, military, and economic empire that Malcolm X threatened with violent revolution has changed over time, as Sunaina Maira observes: contemporary "imperialism is marked by invisibility, secrecy, and flexibility in its operation of power, and by nebulous, nonterritorial forms of domination that do not resemble traditional forms of territorial 'colonialism.'"[13] Today, US imperial power goes well beyond conventional occupation. Its military component is sustained by approximately eight hundred military bases along with a triad of superior air, land, and sea forces.[14] They are an essential component of the government's foundational commitment to the preponderance of US global power, which has been the policy of both Democratic and Republican administrations since Harry S. Truman.[15]

Keeping the US commitment to global military dominance front and center explains why US democracy failed Muslim Americans and others not only during the Cold War but also in its aftermath. In the late twentieth century, the Islamophobic gaze of Americans turned away from Black Muslims as a primary national security threat. The US nation-state and its policymakers, law enforcement officers, political lobbies and think tanks, intelligence agencies, and other centers of power focused instead on "foreign" Muslims inside America. Chapter 4 explains this geopolitical transformation as US political institutions increasingly worried about the threat of transnational political Islam. Conservative political activists and liberal scholars alike worried about what they saw as a tension between Muslim Americans' links to the global community of Muslims, on the one hand, and their commitment to the US nation-state on the other. Could Muslim Americans be loyal to both? Were they able to accept the liberal bargain of operating within the legal and political constraints of the US nation-state?

Rather than analyzing Muslim American participation in electoral politics or another formal realm of politics, chapter 4 offers an ethnographic lens on the lives and thoughts of four Muslim American women, all of whom were living in Jordan at the time I interviewed them in 2009 and 2010. As the chapter shows, gender played an especially central role in how Americans thought about Muslim identity. For many non-Muslim Americans, one of the most visible signs of a foreign presence, transformed into a political fetish, was the veil. After 9/11, Muslim American women, especially those who wore head scarves, came to occupy what Juliane Hammer has called "center stage" in public discourse on Islam.[16] I was interested in discovering whether these women's residency in Jordan transformed their attitudes toward the United States and their identities as Muslims, and I discovered how gender played a role in both questions. Careful to express clear loyalty to the US nation-state, these four women also refused to abandon a sense of solidarity with other communities, including the global community of Muslims and especially Palestinians. Rather than seeing these identities as contradictory or confused, all four women argued that such plural identifications were ethical and rational and expressed the deepest ideals of both Islam and America, including the liberal idea of gender equality. In so doing, these Muslim Americans also imagined a world in which a binary political view of Islam versus the West, the view so dominant in both liberal and conservative US politics, could be transformed and perhaps reconciled. They embraced a form of liberalism that would no longer be tied to war-making in Muslim lands. But they also felt the need to defend or explain Islam's views on women, and it became apparent how

powerful the discourse of liberal intervention on behalf of women remained in their lives.

Chapter 5 then reveals a very different reaction to the challenges of
Muslim American political participation after 9/11. One ultimate sign of
political assimilation is the willingness of citizens to sacrifice themselves
in battle for their nation. It is so central to nation-making that such sacrifices become the stuff of songs, memorials, and even myths. In the US
presidential elections of 2008 and 2016, the blood of two fallen soldiers
named Khan became part of a new American myth that might be called
the myth of the fallen Muslim American soldier. This chapter explores
how US politicians, including Colin Powell and Hillary Clinton, employed the memories of Kareem Khan and Humayun Khan to renew devotion to the ideals of a liberal, multicultural America. I argue, however,
that in focusing on the incorporation of foreign Muslims into the nation,
politicians such as Powell and Clinton offered an ambiguous embrace.

By emphasizing the importance of gaining Muslim American support
in the war against terrorism, US politicians pointed to the very liminality of Muslim Americans. Muslim Americans were part "us" and part
"them." Somewhat suspect—valuable precisely because of their nearness to the enemy—Muslim American service members gave their own
blood in an embodied testimony that the US war on terror was just and
right. Muslim American participation in the US-led war on terror and
Muslim American attempts to support US military, political, and economic intervention in Black and brown nation-states simultaneously
othered Muslim Americans, evoking not only empathy and admiration
among non-Muslims but also orientalist ambivalence. It is hardly surprising, then, that such efforts did little to quell popular violence and
government oppression against Muslims.

The conclusion then considers how the fates of Muslims and America
are tied in our current moment, contemplating how the destiny of US
democracy will depend on what some have called "the Muslim question." I analyze the activism of Muslim American community organizer
and Women's March cochair Linda Sarsour as an example of how Mus-

lim Americans can challenge some of the most powerful, conventional bipartisan platforms of contemporary US politics while also pledging their allegiance to the country and its liberal ideals.

This book thus ends as it begins—as a jeremiad. It critiques the failures of US democracy and points to the failures of liberalism as a key cause. But just beneath the surface of my lament is the hope that American democracy can become something different. The book's moral vision—its "bias"—is born from a desire to see an American community in which Muslims, and all people who have been victimized by American democracy, can flourish and live without the fear of social, political, or economic discrimination. That moral vision is rooted in the idea of a "beloved community" that embraces social equity, justice for all, and peaceful conflict resolution. Solving the problem of Muslim political assimilation offers important signposts along the road to that kind of democracy.

1

The Political Assimilation of Muslim Americans

Rep. André Carson, who represents the Seventh District of the State of Indiana in the 116th US Congress, is an American politician who happens to be Muslim.

According to the biography on his official webpage, he is "a rising member of House leadership." In the 116th US Congress, which convened in January 2019, Representative Carson serves "as a Senior Whip for the House Democratic Caucus," which means that he is expected, when the time comes, to "whip votes"—that is, to ensure that members of his political party vote the way that the Democratic leadership wants them to. In addition, he is chair of the Counterterrorism, Counterintelligence, and Counterproliferation Subcommittee of the Permanent Select Committee on Intelligence.[1] Carson's voting record has been noteworthy for his support of government transparency, and he cosponsored more bills than any other member of the Indiana delegation to the House in the 114th Congress, which ended in early 2017, according to the nonpartisan GovTrack site.[2] Many of Representative Carson's political positions are unsurprising for a congressional Democrat. He supports reducing the cost of college tuition and increasing grants to college students. He introduced the Transition-to-Success Mentoring Act, which would provide coaching and mentoring to at-risk schoolchildren. Representative Carson is in favor of additional federal funding for job training and generally opposes giving presidents fast-track authority to negotiate trade deals. He supports the Neighborhood Revitalization Program, which provides funding to rebuild dilapidated homes. Like most Democrats, he opposes cuts to social security and Medicare. He supports women's reproductive rights, and he has authored legislation designed to bolster veterans' well-being, especially related to mental health. On foreign affairs, Carson has been a strong supporter of counterterrorism military operations in Iraq, Syria, and Afghanistan, while also advocating for the Iran nuclear deal and a two-state solution to the Israeli-Palestinian conflict.[3]

Coming from a district that incorporates much of the city of Indianapolis, Representative Carson largely reflects the political orientation of his voters. Indiana's Seventh District is "solidly Democratic," according to *Roll Call*. Almost a third of the district is African American and 10 percent of constituents are Latinx, but it is still a majority-white district. Carson does not lean strongly to the left or the right.[4] GovTrack ranked him the most liberal member of Indiana's House of Representatives in 2016, but this says very little when considering the composition of Indiana's House delegation and the Republican Party's domination of state politics.[5] For the sake of comparison, note that Carson is ranked the eighty-fifth most progressive member of the House by Progressive-Punch, whose ranking algorithm considers factors such as aid to the disadvantaged, education, the environment, fair taxation, family planning, regulation of corporations, health care, housing, human rights, labor rights, and war and peace. He merits only a "C" or "acceptable" grade as a progressive based on this metric.[6]

Born in Indianapolis in 1974, André Carson became a member of Congress in a 2008 special election held to fill the seat vacated by his grandmother, Rep. Julia Carson, who died the previous year of lung cancer. More than ten politicians had expressed interest in the seat, but Carson won the Democratic Party's nod and then took 53 percent of the vote in a March 11 special election.[7] He was a member of the Indianapolis City-County Council from 2007 to 2008, but before becoming a politician, Carson's career was in law enforcement. For several years, he served as a compliance officer for the Indiana State Excise Police, part of Indiana's Alcohol and Tobacco Commission, and then joined the antiterrorism division of the Indiana Department of Homeland Security. During this time, he was also working toward a college degree. In 2003, he received a B.A. in criminal justice and management from Concordia

University Wisconsin, and in 2005, he took a master's degree in business administration from Indiana Wesleyan University.[8]

By his own account, Carson had a difficult childhood. He did not know his biological father, and his mother was mentally ill. "My mother suffered from schizophrenia, so my grandmother raised me," he said in a 2014 interview.[9] Carson was sent to Saint Rita Catholic School and attended both Tabernacle Missionary Baptist Church and Calvary Temple in Indianapolis. In the 1980s and early 1990s, he became interested in Islam though the music and culture of hip-hop, particularly through those artists who were either members of or influenced by the teachings of the Nation of Islam (NOI) or the Nation of Gods and Earths, otherwise known as the Five Percent Nation or Five Percenters.[10] In particular, Carson loved the music of Rakim Allah. But he did more than consume the music. He created it.

"Rep. Rapper," as he was later dubbed, wrote his first song at the age of ten. Becoming both a break-dancer and MC, Carson developed a local and regional reputation in his teenage years as the artist called Juggernaut. As Juggernaut, Carson never backed down from a verbal throw-down, often engaging in "freestyle rap confrontations" in school hallways. Victory required hard rhetorical work, and the thesaurus and dictionary were his constant companions. During performances as a teen, he would wear "a white-and-blue Adidas jumpsuit"; his hair was parted or had waves, "with my name on the back of my head [and] sometimes a Nike swoosh." Over time, Carson's songs became more socially conscious, addressing drug abuse, government corruption, and class issues.[11] Many years later, as a member of Congress, Carson convened panels on hip-hop and politics for the annual meeting of the Congressional Black Caucus. He said it was a way to expand political participation in the United States and to include the voices of hip-hop artists, activists, and fans in legislation. "I think you need outside agitation and inside instigation to create the necessary friction to bring forth change," Carson told Indianapolis DJ Kyle Long in a 2015 *Nuvo* interview. "When you have those seemingly opposing views that are working at cross purposes you see change. I think change is going to come from the outside critique with the activist community pushing politicians to do better and to think more seriously about the language contained inside legislation."[12]

Like many other urban teenagers who first became interested in Islam via hip-hop, Carson would eventually convert to Sunni Islam. He rejected the theology of the Nation of Islam, which proclaimed a man, W. D. Fard Muhammad, to be God in the flesh, and the teachings of the Five Percenters, who hold that all Black men are gods. Carson married educator Mariama Shaheed, the daughter of Marion County judge and Sunni Muslim David Shaheed. He became a member of Nur Allah Islamic Center, the religious congregation associated with the teachings of the late African American Sunni imam W. D. Mohammed. Carson declared himself to be an "Orthodox, universal, secular" Muslim as questions were raised in his first congressional campaign about potential links to Minister Louis Farrakhan, who delivered a eulogy at his grandmother's funeral. Carson won over local Jewish leaders with his strong support of Israel in Congress—to the consternation of most Muslims, he voted for a congressional resolution supporting the Israeli attack on Gaza in 2008.[13] Over the years, however, he has expressed greater concern for Palestinian self-determination and especially the suffering of people living in Gaza. His position on Israeli-Palestinian affairs, like that of many other younger Democrats, comes closest to the politically moderate J Street lobby—which endorses Carson and encourages Jews to donate to his campaign.[14]

Carson's approach to Islam in the public square echoes the First Amendment's balance of neither establishing a religion for the United States nor preventing the people from freely exercising their religion. "The founders were very visionary when they said there should be no religious test to hold public office," Carson once explained, "because there can be a danger when politicians use their public office to proselytize, and to ostracize people who don't feel the same way as them." He will not discuss how often he prays, and he has even declined questions about whether he consumes alcohol.[15] But Representative Carson is not shy about discussing how the ethics of Islam inspire him as a legislator.

Echoing the message of so many Muslim Americans, Carson sees Islamic and American values as complementary, not contradictory. When explaining how Islamic values inspire his political platform, he sometimes cites the Qur'an and hadith, or the reports of the words and deeds of the Prophet Muhammad and his companions. For example, in discussing whether one could support women's equality as a Muslim, Carson has explained that "it was the Prophet Mohammed, peace be upon him, who stated explicitly in the Hadith that a man who educates his daughters is granted paradise. I think that has figurative implications and political implications." In his struggle for racial equality he is similarly inspired by the Prophet Muhammad: "In the Prophet's last sermon he said there is no superiority—white over black, Arab over non-Arab— words that were quite visionary and also applicable to our times today." Though times have changed—Carson once joked that the invention of toilet paper had abrogated the need to use stones, as the Prophet sometimes did—certain universal values could still apply to policymaking as long as it was practicable to do so. In discussing the Affordable Care Act, Obama's signature domestic legislative effort to reform health care, Carson said that "one of the Islamic tenets is charity and giving to the less fortunate. The United States is arguably the wealthiest nation in recorded history, a country whose healthcare is a large part of its GDP [gross domestic product]. Solving the problem of healthcare relieves a lot of those budgetary issues, but also sees the less fortunate in my community get help." He argues that though institutional bigotry poses a challenge for Muslims who wish to participate in US society, the best remedy is to organize politically and increase grassroots participation.[16]

Considering his upbeat view on America and Islam, his careful political positions on controversial issues such as Israel-Palestine, his legislative priorities, his winsome personality, and his general popularity—he won with 65 percent of the vote in the 2018 election—one might reasonably assume that Carson's Muslim identity would not raise concerns on

Capitol Hill or among more than a few crackpots. How could he be any more assimilated, any more American? Though his grandmother was a member of Congress, Carson did not inherit a fortune, and he has not enriched himself since becoming a member himself—in fact, he was one of the poorest members of the 115th Congress and had a negative net worth.[17] His is the story of a once-homeless child who worked his way through school as a law enforcement officer—surely that quintessentially bootstrapping tale would insulate him from the wild claims of bigoted Islamophobes.

But it has not.

In 2015, when House Democratic leader Nancy Pelosi selected Carson to serve on the House Intelligence Committee—a natural fit given his experience as a former counterterrorism official in Indiana government—right-wing pundits and media interpreted the event as an existential assault on the United States. *The Daily Caller* said that Carson had "received political contributions from Islamist groups named as unindicted co-conspirators of terrorist organizations." Similarly, *Breitbart* claimed there had been donations of $34,000 from "Islamist" sources.[18] On February 6, 2015, professional Islamophobe Frank Gaffney published a "dossier" that fabricated "Rep. Carson's long history of associating with organizations known to be front groups for the Muslim Brotherhood [the Egyptian political party now repressed by the Egyptian government]."[19] The ironically named Religious Freedom Coalition declared that "it is wholly unacceptable to have as a member of a key congressional committee charged with overseeing US intelligence and counterintelligence an individual with extensive personal and political associations with the Muslim Brotherhood's civilization jihadist infrastructure in America." Because of Carson's (imaginary) associations, state secrets could fall into the hands of the enemy, it was said.[20] In 2016, Sen. Ted Cruz of Texas invited testimony from a conspiracy theorist in front of the US Senate Judiciary Subcommittee on Oversight, Agency Action, Federal Rights and Federal Courts; in sworn testimony, the man said that Carson and Rep. Keith Ellison (D-Minnesota), the first Muslim elected to Congress, had ties to terrorist groups. "Allegations that Ellison and Carson are secret Muslim agents with extremist leanings are usually found among fringe groups online, often discussed in dire tones on poorly designed websites," noted reporters Sam Stein and Jessica Schulberg. "Rarely, if ever, do such sentiments get read into congressional testimony, with the imprimatur that offers."[21]

By 2016, however, Sen. Ted Cruz's openly Islamophobic views were no longer so unusual in his party. From 2002 to 2016, the number of Republican or Republican-leaning Americans who thought that at least some, about half, or almost all US Muslims were anti-American jumped from 47 to 63 percent.[22] The number of Democrats worried about anti-Americanism among US Muslims declined in this era. Those Republicans most concerned about Islamic extremism said, by a significant margin, that either Donald Trump or Ted Cruz would make a good president. The correlation makes sense in light of the fact that many of Trump's and Cruz's advisers on Islam and Muslims were the very same Islamophobes who concocted the fantasy that Muslim Rep. Carson is secretly controlled by a foreign Muslim cabal, that he is the "Manchurian Candidate" of the Muslim Brotherhood. Since 9/11, professional anti-Muslim critics and activists such as Gaffney, Pamela Geller, and Robert Spencer have helped to produce a body of Islamophobic, conspiratorial fictions built on racist assumptions and half-truths.[23] Their sophomoric attempts to "connect the dots" linking a sitting member of Congress to anti-American terrorists are irrational and unfounded, but they have been effective in helping politicians such as Trump and Cruz instrumentalize prejudice and hatred for the purposes of partisan gain.

Such anti-Muslim bias has consequences in terms of how many Muslims can run for and be elected to office, and Muslims remain underrepresented in the US Congress. All things being equal, if approximately 1 percent of the US adult population is Muslim, one might expect that 5 or 6 of the 535 members of Congress (including both the House of Representatives and the Senate) would be as well. Other religious minorities have been better represented. The 115th Congress included three Buddhists and three Hindus, even though Buddhists and Hindus represent smaller shares of the US population than do Muslims. The thirty Jewish members of Congress represented 5.6 percent of all federal legislators, though Jews were only 1.9 percent of the adult US population. Like Jews, Christians were also overrepresented in the body. A whopping 90.7 percent of the 115th Congress, 485 members, identified as Christian, even though only 71 percent of US adults do. Americans with no religious affiliation, who were 23 percent of the adult US population, were almost as rare as Muslim members.[24] Addressing the question of why there have been so few Muslims in Congress, political scientist Abdelkader Sinno argues that "the combined effect of a majoritarian system [versus proportional representation], large [congressional] districts, and hostility to Muslim candidates" explains the underrepresentation of Muslims better than any monocausal explanation. Sinno also documents the efforts of political lobbies and public interest groups in opposing Muslim candidates.[25]

Whatever factors are driving Muslim underrepresentation, the career of Representative Carson is reflective of a broader Muslim American desire to participate in politics.[26] In the 2018 election cycle, over ninety Muslim candidates ran for a variety of offices—Deedra Abboud to be US senator from Arizona and Jesse Sbaih to be US senator from Nevada; Abdul El-Sayed to be governor of Michigan; and Nadia Hashimi of Maryland, Sameena Mustafa of Illinois, and Fayrouz Saad of Michigan, to be members of the House of Representatives.[27] Among these candidates, Minnesota State House Rep. Ilhan Omar, a Somali refugee, and Rashida Tlaib, a Palestinian American from Michigan, won their contests, becoming the first two Muslim women elected to the US House of Representatives.

American- and foreign-born Muslims have also served in state legislatures across the country, mainly as members of the Democratic Party. These legislators have included North Carolina State Senator Larry Shaw, first elected to the North Carolina House in 1994; New Hampshire Rep. Saghir "Saggy" Tahir, a Republican elected in 2000; Missouri State Rep.

Yaphett El-Amin, elected in 2002 and succeeded by her husband, T. D. El-Amin, in 2006; Saqib Ali, elected to the Maryland House of Delegates in 2006; and Ako Abdul-Samad, elected to the Iowa House in 2006.[28]

In addition, Muslims have held prominent positions in the White House and elsewhere in federal government. Some of the more prominent officials include Elias Zerhouni, director of the National Institutes of Health from 2002 to 2008; Zalmay Khalilzad, US ambassador to Afghanistan, then to Iraq, and finally to the United Nations during George W. Bush's presidency; Farah Pandith, a national security official in George W. Bush's White House and later the US State Department special representative to Muslim communities under Barack Obama; and Huma Abedin, deputy chief of staff to Secretary of State Hillary Clinton and vice chair of Clinton's 2016 campaign for the presidency.[29]

Though the number of Muslim Americans elected to formal political office is modest, Muslim Americans have been cultivating other forms of political participation since the antebellum era, testifying to a desire to have a political voice in the destiny of Muslims both in the United States and abroad. To name a few examples: In 1828, formerly enslaved West African prince Abdul Rahman Ibrahima toured the country as an antislavery speaker and visited President John Quincy Adams at the White House, a visit that became fodder for the partisans of Andrew Jackson. It was said that Adams's support of Ibrahima was evidence that Adams would threaten the legality of slavery in the South.[30] Hundreds of Muslims served in the armed forces of both the Union and Confederacy during the Civil War (1861–1865); perhaps the most prominent of them was African-born polyglot Nicholas Said, who volunteered for the Massachusetts Fifty-Fifth (Colored) Infantry.[31] President Grover Cleveland's counsel to the Philippines, Democratic newspaperman Alexander Russell Webb, converted to Islam while he was serving in Manila and later represented all Muslims at the Parliament of Religions at the Chicago World's Fair in 1893.[32] Then, after World War I, Muslims began to organize more formal civic groups, participating in debates about foreign policy issues such as the US position on Zionism.[33] For much of US history, Muslims have remained a small percentage of the population—and, more importantly, generally did not attract the attention of national media and the federal government. This lack of awareness about the long history of Muslim Americans may contribute to the sense that they are new to US politics—or even that they have not wanted to get involved.

As we will see, Muslim American politics became more visible to the general public after World War II, when the Nation of Islam emerged as a nationally and internationally known voice of political dissent. What has been little noticed is the other major postwar political trend among Muslim Americans. Arab American Muslims, a religious minority in the Arab American community at the time, were increasingly participating in local political life as white ethnics. Their status as white people was always unstable, and much of that privilege would be taken away after 9/11, but the 1950s were different from today. Muslims were seen as potential allies in the Cold War. Republican president and former Allied commander Dwight D. Eisenhower and his vice president, Richard M. Nixon, saw belief in God as central to the ideological struggle against communism and its spread in the developing world. During this era, the words "under God" were added to the Pledge of Allegiance, and "In God we Trust" was adopted as the national motto. Drawing on the central myth of American exceptionalism that began with the Massachusetts Bay Colony, Eisenhower claimed that the whole system of American government "makes no sense unless it is founded on a deeply held religious belief, and I don't care what that is."[34] In cities such as Detroit, Michigan, and Toledo, Ohio, mosques that had been established in the interwar period provided institutional platforms from which Muslim Americans became politically active and civically engaged. Echoing the ideology of President Eisenhower and the liberal consensus in general, weekend religious teachers stressed how Islamic religion and US nationalism were complementary—being Muslim made one a better American, and being American made one a better Muslim.[35]

While Nation of Islam members and later some Sunni and Shi'a Muslims avoided voting and participating in US politics, other Muslims have always taken part in local, state, and federal elections when allowed to do so. The stigmatization of Muslim Americans as a foreign, alien presence, particularly after 9/11, has obscured better understanding of the robust efforts among Muslim American activists and community leaders to increase the impact of Muslim Americans in US elections and politics more generally. It is important to recognize these attempts of Muslim Americans to assimilate into US society via politics. Especially when Muslim Americans are constantly imagined as exceptional, charting the normalcy of their political participation is essential to a critique of the limitations of US democracy in our era.

Muslim American Political Participation in the Twenty-First Century

Since 9/11, Muslim Americans have become reliable Democratic voters. Looking at Muslim American politics from the point of view of the late twentieth century, this was no foregone conclusion. African American Muslim leader Imam W. D. Mohammed supported Republican president George H. W. Bush. Arab and South Asian American Muslim endorsements for George W. Bush may have tipped the state of Florida to him.[36] But it became unusual for any popular Muslim American leader to endorse Republican presidential candidates after 2000. According to a 2017 Pew poll, Muslim Americans "from a wide variety of social and demographic backgrounds express a preference for the Democratic Party over the GOP," and that support has been consistent since the presidential election of 2004.[37] In the post-9/11 era, Muslim American voters decided that the Democratic candidate—especially when it was Barack Obama—addressed their concerns, particularly about anti-Muslim discrimination, more effectively.

One way to measure Muslim American political participation is to examine the percentage of eligible voters who say that they actually showed up to vote. About four out of every five Muslims in the United States are US citizens. Of those citizens, 44 percent of eligible Muslim voters told Pew that they voted in the presidential election of 2016—a significantly smaller percentage than the national average of 58 percent participation by eligible voters. One-third of Muslim Americans polled by the Institute for Social Policy and Understanding said they did not vote because they "didn't like any of the people running." Another third said they were not registered to vote or were unavailable or unable to vote.[38] While 54 percent of US-born Muslims voted in 2016, only 37 percent of foreign-born, naturalized Muslim citizens said that they did so. Among the factors that may explain this discrepancy are the increased fear of government repression among foreign-born Muslims and the fear generated through anti-Muslim political rhetoric, discrimination, and hate crimes that targeted immigrant Muslim people and places of worship in the months before the election.

Whatever the main reason for the lower-than-average voter turnout, Islamic religion was not a significant factor. Only 3 percent reported not voting because it was "against their religion."[39] On the contrary, Islamic religiosity has been associated in the twenty-first century with greater political and civic participation. According to political scientists Karam Dana, Bryan Wilcox Archuleta, and Matt Barreto, who administered over fourteen hundred surveys in twenty-two different locations to understand the relationship between Islam and politics, Muslims who reported attending mosque more frequently, studying the Qur'an and the hadith, and engaging in Islamic philanthropy were more likely to believe in the compatibility of American democracy and Islamic religion and more likely to participate in various forms of nonelectoral politics. "Quite simply," as the authors put it, "the most religious are the most likely to believe in political integration in the United States."[40]

As religious studies scholar Farida Jalalzai has argued, race, ethnicity, and nativity are also significant factors shaping Muslim American political participation. Most African American Muslims are US-born, and, like other American-born Muslims, they are much more likely than foreign-born Muslims to be politically engaged. "Native born respondents have more potential exposure to American political processes, ultimately paying attention to and participating more in politics," she argues. Contrariwise, South Asian American Muslims "are the least participatory of ethnic/racial subgroups in rally attendance, media writing and petition singing, navigating political websites and following politics." Arab American Muslims are in between.[41]

The current political behavior of Muslim Americans thus reflects, in part, the degree to which each racial or ethnic group has historical roots in American politics. The leading role of African American Muslims in both grassroots activism and US political life in the twenty-first century seems expected given the participation of African Americans in the unfolding of American political ideas, platforms, organizations, and elections since the 1800s. This is Rep. André Carson's explanation for why the first two Muslims elected to Congress were African Americans from the Midwest: "What you are seeing from Representative Ellison and myself are Muslims that come from the African American experience. We are more concerned with civil and human rights, with education, with the global economy, creating jobs and how to repair broken infrastructure. These are issues Midwesterners relate to."[42] Similarly, Arab Americans developed formal civic and ethnic associations with an eye toward political participation in the first half of the twentieth century. Even though the majority of contemporary Arab American Muslims trace their ancestry to post-1965 immigration, these Arabic-speaking Muslims landed in a place where two to three generations of other Arabic speakers had already been building cultural, political, and economic capital.[43] Religion—as well as national origin, language, class, and race—is often a source of division in Arab American communities, but social networks, business ties, and political organizing can cross such divides. As a result, a significant number of Arab American Muslims have sought Arab American Christian partners to oppose immigration measures targeting people from Arabic-speaking countries, to support the cause of Palestinian self-determination, to challenge both anti-Arab and anti-Muslim stereotypes, and to build intersectional alliances with other oppressed populations in the United States.[44] Given that Muslims constitute but 1 percent of the US population, such alliances seem to be another sign that Muslim political activists, like non-Muslim political activists, recognize the importance of coalition building for effective political participation.

Another powerful sign of Muslim American political assimilation into the United States is the Muslim American belief in political ideals such as freedom, liberty, equality under law, equality of opportunity, and patriotism. To cite just two illustrative examples for now, according to the 2017 Pew poll, 92 percent of all Muslims reported that they were proud to be American (compared to 91 percent of the general public). And sometimes Muslims are bigger boosters of America than non-Muslims. Of all Muslims surveyed, 70 percent agreed that people in the United States "can get ahead through hard work" compared to only 62 percent of the general public who believed in "the American dream."[45] Taking these statements on their face value, and assuming at the very least that they express a desire for acceptance, the refusal of some Americans to recognize, celebrate, and accept the assimilationist behavior of Muslim Americans seems particularly senseless.[46] No matter how assimilated Muslims become, their acceptance within US society has remained precarious.

Islamophobia and the Rejection of Muslim American Assimilation

For many Muslim Americans, the evidence that, no matter what they do, they will not be allowed to assimilate in the United States is deeply felt. Voting and other forms of political participation take place in a larger social and cultural context in which many Muslim Americans feel unsafe. Anti-Muslim activity can take a variety of forms, according to the Muslim Diaspora Initiative of the New America public research group, which documented 675 such incidents from 2012 through the first quarter of 2018. These activities included opposition to refugee resettlement; opposition to Muslim mosques, cemeteries, and schools; anti-Muslim statements and behavior by elected officials; and anti-Muslim violence.[47] Hate crimes—that is, attacks against person or property motivated by the hatred of a person's identity—are the most chilling example of how some Americans refuse to accept the presence of Muslims in their midst. In 2016, during a presidential campaign season in which anti-Muslim rhetoric played a large role, the Federal Bureau of Investigation (FBI) reported the highest-ever number of physical assaults against Muslim Americans: 127. Since 2001, there have been nearly 900 reported assaults against Muslims. According to the Pew Research Center, "the FBI collects hate crime data from about 15,000 law enforcement agencies that voluntarily participate, which means the annual statistics likely undercount the number of hate crimes in a given year."[48]

Hate crimes victimize the entire community, creating terror as stories of anti-Muslim violence are circulated both in national and international media and among formal and informal networks of Muslims in the United States. For example, the 2015 murders of Deah Barakat, twenty-three years old, Yusor Abu-Salha, twenty-one, and Razan Abu-Salha, nineteen, in Chapel Hill, North Carolina, are remembered across the country as heartbreaking anti-Muslim crimes. On February 10, a forty-six-year-old neighbor, Craig Hicks, shot all three of them in the head; the sisters were killed execution style. Hicks was a libertarian who often carried a gun while berating fellow residents about their violations of parking rules. He also stared at his female Muslim neighbors' head scarves, making them feel like he did not like them. Whatever he was thinking or feeling when he executed his young neighbors, Muslims around the country experienced it as an attack on the promise of belonging in and to America. Barakat and Yusor Abu-Salaha were newlyweds; Razan Abu-Salha was Yusor's sister. Barakat, a North Carolina State (NCSU) graduate, was in his second year at UNC Dentistry School, where his wife, who also graduated from NCSU, hoped to join him. Razan was a sophomore at NCSU. They were committed to community service and international relief, and for many, they represented the best of Muslim America.[49]

Their loss evoked more than grief. It confirmed the fear that Muslims were unsafe in America just because they were Muslim. In the 2017 Pew poll, 6 percent of all Muslims interviewed reported being physically threatened or attacked—130,000 people out of an adult population of 2.15 million. Muslim Americans reasonably fear that a threat could escalate into physical assault, especially in an environment in which 32 percent of all Muslims report that, in the past year, someone had acted as if they were suspicious of them.[50] Such fears are also reasonable given that Islam is consistently rated as the least popular American religion: one-quarter of all Americans tell pollsters that a majority of Muslim Americans are anti-American, and 41 percent say that Islam encourages more violence than other religions.[51] It is thus all the more remarkable that Muslim Americans do not feel alienated from the United States. Four out of every five are satisfied with the ways things are going in their lives, and 55 percent think that Americans are generally friendly toward Muslims.[52] For most Muslim Americans, the problem is not American ideals, the American dream, or American people; the problem is anti-Muslim discrimination.

In understanding the nature of anti-Muslim bias, discrimination, and violence, researchers from a variety of disciplines have stressed that what is commonly called Islamophobia is not only the product of individual and popular ignorance and hatred but also of institutions and structures such as public policies, policing, media, political lobbying, and so on.[53] In 2017, for example, federal agencies were responsible for 35 percent of all anti-Muslim bias incidents documented in the Council of American-Islamic Relation's 2018 civil rights report. The agency most responsible for this anti-Muslim discrimination, partly because of President Trump's three attempts to ban visitors from selected Muslim-majority countries, was US Customs and Border Protection, but the Transportation Security

Administration, the FBI, US Citizenship and Immigration Services, and US Immigration and Customs Enforcement, among other agencies, also contributed to this pattern. A total of 5,650 bias reports were made to CAIR, and organization staff verified that 2,599 "contained an identifiable element of religious, ethnic, or national origin bias." In addition to government-based discrimination, CAIR documented harassment, hate crimes, and employment discrimination in various sites ranging from air, bus, and train terminals to homes and schools.[54]

The American Civil Liberties Union similarly argues that the freedom of Muslim Americans is violated by the federal and state governments through policies related to national security profiling, federal watch lists, and the Countering Violent Extremism (CVE) program. National security profiling includes the collection of "racial and ethnic information," which is then developed into maps according to "crude stereotypes about which groups commit different types of crimes." The government also maintains terrorist watch lists that designate individuals who are to be frequently interrogated by law enforcement; some of them are placed on the "no fly list," which has been ruled by one judge to violate the constitutional right of due process. In addition, the government encourages citizens to "say something if they see something," and the mere appearance of a young man wearing a skullcap and reading the Qur'an on an airplane can be reported as a terrorist threat. Similarly, the CVE program symbolically deputizes religious leaders, social workers, and teachers in this effort, asking them to report individuals under their supervision who have radical views. One can hardly imagine a better example of how federal law enforcement encourages citizens to be afraid of and discriminate against Muslims.[55]

The FBI also plays a significant role in stoking Islamophobia through its counterintelligence operations. In its $8.77 billion 2018 budget request to the US Congress, Andrew McCabe, then acting director of the bureau, testified that "preventing terrorist attacks remains the FBI's top priority." The bureau was focused primarily on the following: "(1) those who are inspired by terrorist propaganda and feel empowered to act out in support; (2) those who are enabled to act after gaining inspiration from extremist propaganda and communicating with members of foreign terrorist organizations who provide guidance on operational planning or targets; and (3) those who are directed by members of foreign terrorist organizations to commit specific, directed acts in support of the group's ideology or cause."[56] The FBI conducts many of its antiterrorism investigations in the Muslim American community; a little more than half of all terrorism prosecutions from 9/11 until 2016 involved Muslims, while the rest involved right-wing, left-wing, and other groups.[57]

In addition to conducting surveillance on Muslims, the FBI runs elaborate sting operations to ferret out "potential" Muslim terrorists. Though generally regarded by federal US courts as legal prosecutorial techniques, these sting operations are a form of entrapment, which "in a more general sociological sense can be said to occur whenever a government agent or informant is involved in bringing about the commission of an offence."[58] In running a sting operation, the FBI identifies a person of interest using its network of perhaps fifteen thousand informants, some of whom can be paid as much as $100,000 per case. Investigative journalist Trevor Aaronson summarizes what often happens next: "Informants report to their handlers on people who have, say, made statements sympathizing with terrorists. Those names are then cross-referenced with existing intelligence data, such as immigration and criminal records. FBI agents may then assign an undercover operative to approach the target by posing as a radical. Sometimes the operative will propose a plot, provide explosives, even lead the target in a fake oath to al-Qaeda. Once enough incriminating information has been gathered, there's an arrest—and a press conference announcing another foiled plot."[59] The people who have been stung constitute a significant source of the FBI's total number of terrorism prosecutions. According to a *New York Times* investigation, 67 percent of all such prosecutions from February 2015 to July 2016 were the result of undercover operations.[60] From 2001 to 2014, according to a report by Human Rights Watch, "nearly 50 percent of the more than 500 federal counterterrorism convictions resulted from informant-based cases."[61] Similarly, criminologist Jesse Norris and sociologist Hanna Grol-Prokopczyk found that out of 580 cases since 9/11, about 55 percent, or 317, involved an informant or undercover agent. Moreover, though the FBI used entrapment in a variety of terrorism investigations, including the investigation of right-wing extremism, Muslims were far more likely than non-Muslims to be the victims of a sting operation.[62]

Many Muslim Americans argue that these prosecutorial approaches do more harm than good. As Human Rights Watch points out, they alienate "the very communities the government relies on most to report possible terrorist threats and divert resources from other, more effective ways of responding to the threats of terrorism."[63] Norris and Grol-Prokopczyk recommend that the government stop trying to "coax law-abiding citizens into terrorist schemes"; a more constructive approach would require that the FBI "have a reasonable suspicion of criminal activity before inducing a suspect into committing a crime."[64]

The ultimate political rejection of Muslim American assimilation is the abuse and torture of Muslim bodies by the state. In 2004, for example, the FBI wrongly accused Oregon attorney and Muslim American Brandon Mayfield, who had served in the US Army Reserve from 1985 to 1989 and as an officer in US Army from 1992 to 1994, of involvement in the Madrid bombings of 2004. The FBI crime lab said that it found Mayfield's print on a plastic bag near the crime scene; the Spanish National Police proved the FBI wrong. During his nineteen days in custody, Mayfield said that he was "subject to lock-down, strip searches, sleep deprivation, unsanitary living conditions, shackles and chains, threats, physical pain, and humiliation." In 2006, the government agreed to pay Mayfield $2 million and issued a formal apology.[65] Similarly, James Yee, a captain in the US Army and Guantanamo Bay Muslim chaplain, was wrongly accused of mutiny, sedition, and spying in 2003. He was kept in solitary confinement in a military brig for seventy-six days and was also subject to sleep deprivation. He was later exonerated and left the army with an honorable discharge in 2005.[66]

These cases are remarkable in that both men had a background in US military service and could still be unjustly accused of terrorism and subjected to human rights abuses. The treatment of non-citizen Muslims by US government institutions has been even worse; indeed, it has been horrific. During the Iraq War, Iraq's Abu Ghraib prison became the setting for systematic sexual abuse and torture. In addition, the CIA tortured potential suspects in extralegal sites or sent them, via extraordinary rendition, to foreign governments who would do it for them.[67] And the creation of a detention facility at Guantanamo Bay allowed the government to detain so-called enemy combatants so that they did not have to treat them as prisoners of war under the Geneva Conventions. This facility drew global opprobrium as multiple, confirmed reports established that the government was subjecting dozens of people to waterboarding, sensory deprivation techniques, and inhumane living conditions, among other human rights violations.[68] Only one of the detainees, Yasser Hamdi, was a US citizen. But whether the Muslims kept there were American or not, their abuse stoked fear and anxiety among Muslims in the United States. Would they be disappeared too?

As the politics of Islamophobia came to be one of the defining characteristics of the US presidential election of 2016, questions about the safety and well-being, about the life and liberty of Muslim Americans prompted Muslims and their non-Muslim allies to ask basic questions about the best political and legal strategies to protect Muslim Americans and advance their interests. The answers to such questions had to grapple in some way with the relationship of Muslim Americans to the liberal bargain that so many had attempted to strike since the late twentieth century. That bargain rested on the assumption that if Muslim Americans were willing to become politically active, work hard, obey the law, reach out to their non-Muslim neighbors, and defend the country with their blood and their treasure, then they would be afforded full legal equality and protections of their rights to property, free assembly, trial by jury, no illegal search or seizure, and the free exercise of their religion. If Muslim Americans would keep the faith with the nation, then assimilation might still be achieved.

But some Muslims from the 1950s through today have pointed to the limits of this liberal bargain and the ways that it too easily sustains racism at home and militarism abroad. Whether these Muslim Americans have been reform-minded critics or radical dissenters, they have identified a core problem of US liberalism and argued for political change. How the US government has responded to that Muslim American challenge indicates the extent to which the nation-state will go to preserve a white supremacist and imperial status quo. This has been clear, as the next chapter argues, at least since the 1950s, when the US sought to repress the first Muslim movement of any sort to offer a popular political alternative to US liberalism. But even that movement did not abandon liberalism completely.

2

The Nation of Islam and the Cold War Liberal Consensus

A Muslim American political vision first became consequential on the national scene not in dreams of assimilation but in an embrace of racial and religious separatism. It was formed pragmatically as a response to a racially segregated country that had been established as a slave republic and, even after slavery ended formally in 1865, was structured along lines of Jim Crow segregation and white racial nationalism. In the 1950s, this Muslim American political voice of dissent was born from the country's Muslim African American converts.

Members of the Nation of Islam became known across the United States for their radical resistance to white supremacy, US foreign policy, Black Christianity, and the liberal dream of racial integration. Because of the movement's dissenting political voice, it became a prime target of US governmental surveillance and repression. The very presence of Elijah Muhammad's new religious movement was perceived as a threat to the ideological foundations of 1960s US liberalism, which rested on anticommunism and the suppression of political dissent both at home and abroad, the rhetoric of equal rights under the law and sometimes of racial integration, and federal welfare programs.[1] Instead, the Nation of Islam advocated racial separatism, Black capitalism, Afro-Asian solidarity, and a cultural and religious identity that revolved around its unique understanding of Islam. Often positioning themselves, like other African American radicals in the 1960s, against US intervention in Africa and Asia, Nation of Islam members celebrated their solidarity with nonaligned leaders, especially the Egyptian president, Gamal Abdel Nasser.

But, as I argue below, the Nation of Islam leadership did not advocate either violent or nonviolent African American involvement in freedom struggles abroad (or, for that matter, at home). They also appropriated and furthered what were at the time several other modes of liberalism: they policed members' middle-class mores and straight sexuality; embraced the dream of Black capitalism and encouraged entrepreneurship; used the US courts to argue for freedom of religion and framed the Nation's activities in that light; and forbade members from engaging in violent revolution or even nonviolent political resistance against many of the liberal institutions they identified as religious evils. The presence of these liberalisms within the Nation of Islam renders useless any facile judgments of its radical or conservative nature. Instead, the meaning of liberalism and radicalism in the movement must be understood carefully within the overlapping political, social, and cultural contexts within which the group operated. Rather than judging the movement as either wholly radical, liberal, or conservative, this chapter reveals the ways in which the movement preserved certain elements of liberalism while also challenging its multiple foundations.

Finally, the opposition of liberal ideologues and US government officials to the Nation of Islam demonstrates how, in practice, American democracy was invested, to a greater or lesser degree, in white supremacy and US imperial domination. This chapter shows how regnant forms of US liberalism prevented the assimilation of Muslims into the republic even though the Nation of Islam's religious and political thought reflected a number of liberal elements—from its stance on private wealth accumulation to its use of liberal rhetoric concerning freedom. Instead of remaking American democracy in a way that made public space for the Nation of Islam's advocacy of separate and independent Black institutions and its opposition to US neocolonialism, the nation—its formal institutions and its citizens—cast these Muslims out of the body politic.

The Radical Political Challenge of Elijah Muhammad's Nation of Islam

Elijah Muhammad's Nation of Islam (NOI) played a unique role in a longer history of American and particularly African American cultural, religious, and political engagements with the Middle East and Islam, but it was not the first African American movement to interpret Islamic religion as an English-speaking Black international freedom discourse. This idea had already been established by intellectuals such as Edward Wilmot Blyden, author of *Christianity, Islam, and the Negro Race* (1887), and Dusé Mohamed Ali, editor of the *African Times and Orient Review* and, after World War I, foreign affairs columnist for the Universal Negro Improvement Association's *Negro World*.[2] In the 1920s, the decade during which a variety of Muslim religious congregations and other voluntary associations became institutionalized among African Americans, especially in the Midwest and along the East Coast, one common thread that linked most of the groups popular in places such as Chicago, Detroit, Newark, New York, Pittsburgh, and Saint Louis was the idea that Islamic religion, often in contradistinction to Christianity, nurtured Black political self-determination or at the very least racial equality.[3] This was the case in all Islamic groups popular among African American Muslims, including the Moorish Science Temple, the Ahmadiyya movement, and the Black Sunni Muslim congregations associated with the leadership of Sudanese missionary Satti Majid.[4]

The Nation of Islam, founded by W. D. Fard Muhammad in 1930 as the Temple of Islam in Greater Detroit, was only one of the many Muslim groups established in the interwar period, but it emerged after World War II as the largest single African American Muslim organization, and by the late 1950s it was arguably the most prominent Muslim organization in the United States.[5] Like most other African American Muslim groups, whether Sunni, Ahmadi, or Moorish in religious orientation, the politics of the Nation of Islam linked the struggle for Black dignity, freedom, and self-determination in the United States to the struggles of all people of color abroad, the so-called Dark World. In its rejection of Christianity, racial integration, and other components of liberalism, the Nation of Islam became a radical symbol of anti-Americanism.[6] Unlike many Black radicals who saw an alternative in communism, however, Elijah Muhammad identified Islam as the solution to such problems.

During the 1950s and 1960s, Nation of Islam members would debate, define, and engender this revolutionary Islam in different ways. At least some members, especially Malcolm X, saw Gamal Abdel Nasser, the revolutionary leader of the United Arab Republic (the combined state of Egypt and Syria), as a model and leader of Islamic moral and political engagement. Like others around the world, many African American Muslims and African American leftists hailed Nasser's weathering of the Suez Crisis in 1956. Some members hung pictures of him in their homes.[7] In 1958, the year during which the UAR was formed and Nasser convened a meeting of the Afro-Asian Conference in Cairo, Elijah Muhammad cabled Nasser to seek his support for the NOI. In words that seem to be crafted by Malcolm X, he urged Nasser to see their movements as branches of the same tree. "Freedom, justice, and equality for all Africans and Asians is of far-reaching importance, not only to you of the East, but also to over 17,000,000 of your long-lost brothers of African-Asian descent here in the West," the cable read. The symbolic link between the Nation of Islam and Nasser was so strong by the late 1950s that it prompted Thurgood Marshall, lawyer for the National Association for the Advancement of Colored People (NAACP) and future US Supreme Court justice, to denounce the entire movement in anti-Nasserite terms. Speaking at Princeton University in New Jersey, Marshall claimed that the group was "run by a bunch of thugs organized from prisons and jails, and financed, I am sure, by Nasser or some Arab group." Marshall also argued that the association of a domestic Black Muslim group with a foreign power, especially with Nasser or "some Arab group," was a serious threat to the US Federal Bureau of Investigation.[8]

Indeed, the FBI had been conducting surveillance on Black Muslims and other religious groups since the 1930s, and it had sought via legal means to repress African American Muslim identification and possible cooperation with non-US groups and persons.[9] A secret study called the Survey of Racial Conditions in the United States, code-named RACON, conducted from 1942 to 1943, sought to discover what it deemed "foreign-inspired agitation among the American Negroes." Its scope was so extensive that it included obviously anticommunist groups such as A. Philip Randolph's March on Washington movement, which sought to obtain jobs for African Americans in the US defense industry. The point of this investigation was to determine the "source(s) of the rising tide of black resistance to the wave of racial discrimination unleashed by the national defense program," according to historian Robert A. Hill.[10] But RACON also discovered the rising identification of African Americans with the Japanese Empire, a kernel of African American consciousness planted in the Japanese victory over Russia in 1905 that grew as some African Americans saw in the rise of Japan the possibility of their own freedom from white supremacy and domination. Among the various groups that eventually endorsed the war objectives of Japan were Mittie Maud Lena Gordon's Peace Movement of Ethiopia and Holiness pastor David D. Ervin's Triumph the Church of the New Age, both based in Chicago.[11]

Though Elijah Muhammad may or may not have been associated with these groups, he did oppose African American participation in World War II based partly on the claim that the United States was not his nation—the *Nation* of Islam was. Elijah Muhammad refused to register for the military draft and was indicted on federal charges of sedition. Convicted of a lesser charge, the religious leader was imprisoned from 1943 to 1946. It was a pattern that movement luminaries would repeat over the following decades: the leader's son, Wallace D. Muhammad, went to prison for refusing the draft in the era of the Korean War, and then, most famously, Cassius Marcellus Clay—Muhammad Ali—refused to be inducted during the Vietnam War.[12]

This resistance to US war-making abroad stood in stark contrast to the eager participation of first- and second-generation Muslim immigrants from Africa, Europe, and Asia, especially those of Syrian and Lebanese descent, who joined the military in large numbers and became enthusiastic supporters of American liberalism's promise to free the world's populations from communism.[13] At the same time that the

Nation of Islam rose as a primary platform for political dissent, many Muslim leaders in the Arab American community argued that Islam shared America's values of liberty and freedom. Their largest national organization, much smaller and less prominent than the Nation of Islam, was the Federation of Islamic Associations (FIA). Founded in 1952 by a World War II veteran and subsequently led by two other veterans, the FIA looked to bring Sunni and Shi'a Muslim Americans together, spread a positive view of Islam, and cultivate friendly relations between Muslim-majority nation-states and the United States, among other goals. The group established ties with the United Arab Republic and President Gamal Abdel Nasser in 1959 and then in 1961 with the government of Saudi Arabia. During its annual conventions in the 1950s and 1960s, the FIA celebrated its largely Arab roots alongside its love of American music and dance.[14]

The US government began to pay attention to this group of Muslims as potential allies in the Cold War. Rejecting the Christian confessionalism of Puritans and twentieth-century Christian fundamentalist doctrines, President Dwight Eisenhower's Cold War ideology included Jews and Muslims and all others of "sincere religious belief" in his vision of America as freedom's defender. This is why Eisenhower attended the opening of the Islamic Center of Washington, DC, in 1957. "It is fitting that we re-dedicate ourselves to the peaceful progress of all men under one God," said Eisenhower during the visit. "I should like to assure you, my Islamic [Muslim] friends," the president said, "that under the American Constitution, under American tradition, and in American hearts, this Center, this place of worship is just as welcome as could be a similar edifice of any other religion."[15]

Perhaps needless to say, Eisenhower never visited an African American Muslim congregation. While Arab American Muslim groups succeeded at building political ties and social influence at the local level in places such as New York City, Detroit, and Toledo—and among the diplomatic corps in Washington, DC—there was little doubt that in the

1960s, most Americans who had heard of Muslims equated them with the "Black Muslims," that is, the Nation of Islam. For them, Islam was a form of resistance to anti-Black racism and US militarism.

By this time, Elijah Muhammad's Nation of Islam had stood as a symbol of (nonviolent) resistance to US militarism for more than a decade. What started as a relatively small movement, one of many different groups that were cultivating religious, political, and cultural identities grounded in alternative notions of Black ethnicity, emerged in the postwar period as the most prominent and successful Muslim religious organization among African Americans. It was becoming what historian Penny Von Eschen called "a space—for the most part unthinkable in the Cold War era—for an anti-American critique of the Cold War."[16]

During this era, the FBI adopted more aggressive counterintelligence techniques to repress the movement. FBI informants were placed inside of and recruited from the ranks of the Nation of Islam. In 1956, J. Edgar Hoover, FBI director, authorized the wiretapping of Elijah Muhammad's phones. In 1959, the intelligence gathered as a result of this surveillance was used in a systematic disinformation campaign against the group. For the next several years, the FBI briefed mainstream media outlets such as *U.S. News & World Report*, *Time*, and the *Saturday Evening Post* on its findings. Eventually, the FBI even turned to writing anonymous letters to Elijah Muhammad's wife about his extramarital affairs. The point of the activities, according to a declassified FBI memorandum, was to expose the movement as a fraud and to create dissension in the ranks.[17]

But it was not only the FBI that was worried about the Nation of Islam, as Thurgood Marshall's comment in 1959 revealed. In advocating the establishment of racially separate social and cultural institutions and businesses along with a religion that preached Black superiority—not so hard a sell at a time when Black people were still being Jim Crowed—the Nation of Islam offered an alternative to the postwar liberal vision of a racially integrated country sustained by a strong welfare state. Liberals, both Black and white, were deeply disappointed in the weak, watered-down civil rights bill that majority leader and future President Lyndon B. Johnson managed to pass through the Southern-dominated US Senate in 1958. Their top priority was a federalization of the civil rights campaign, a bill that would provide the federal law enforcement necessary to end Jim Crow segregation in the South. After putting a Northerner in the White House in 1960, liberal hopes were high for more substantive civil rights legislation.[18]

The Nation of Islam was useful in that it could be cited as the offspring of bad race relations; it could be played up as a threat to social stability. The fact that African American liberals such as Thurgood Marshall, Roy Wilkins, and Derrick Bell, all of whom were NAACP officials at the time, so ferociously attacked the Nation of Islam indicates the depth of its challenge. This critique of the group was also adopted by the Rev. Dr. Martin Luther King Jr., who named the Nation of Islam as the "largest" and "best known" Black nationalist movement in the United States in his now-canonical 1963 "Letter from a Birmingham Jail." King tried to make the threat plain to his white audience by arguing that domestic Black nationalism would fan the flames of political violence in the same way that political revolutions were sweeping through the developing world. He said the need for change was urgent. The Nation of Islam was thus appropriated, at times in apocalyptic language, as a symbol of what was to come—James Baldwin's "the fire next time"—unless racial equality was achieved.[19]

The passage of civil rights laws in 1964 and 1965 did not, however, quiet the radical voice of opposition to postwar liberalism. Black youth began to amplify the call for social and political change. For most African Americans, these laws did little to eliminate the presence of de facto racial discrimination—and even in the case of de jure discrimination, only certain elements of Jim Crow segregation were legally dismantled through federal law enforcement and the courts.[20] As it was practiced in the 1960s, American liberalism was what Black studies scholar George

Lipsitz calls a "possessive investment in whiteness," a commitment to the freedom of white people to enjoy life and the pursuit of happiness at the expense of nonwhite people.[21]

In response to liberalism's failure to provide fair housing, jobs, and actual desegregation to people of color, various advocates of Black Power and eventually Black Consciousness began to adopt and adapt the rhetoric and programs of the Nation of Islam, advocating Black pride, community self-defense, separate schools, racially separate businesses, and, perhaps most commonly, opposition to the Vietnam War. Even as various aspects of the movement were rejected as insufficiently radical, Nation of Islam member Muhammad Ali's willingness to give up the heavyweight boxing crown and go to jail rather be inducted into the US Army became a symbol of dissent unmatched in the United States and around the world.[22]

As a result, the FBI still regarded the NOI as a major threat. In 1967, it increased what it described as its "operational intensity" in counterintelligence operations—called COINTELPRO—against the NOI. Targeting "Black Nationalist-Hate Groups," the FBI sought, in Director Hoover's words, "to expose, disrupt, misdirect, discredit, or otherwise neutralize the activities of black nationalist, hate type organizations." In addition to relying on the surveillance and disinformation that it had conducted since the 1950s, the Bureau attempted to create dissension among movement members and spark conflict between the Nation of Islam and the Black Panther Party.[23] In some cases, the agency succeeded in eliminating various Black activist groups, but the Nation of Islam, having dealt with government repression since the 1930s, was able to withstand the interference. Even after the departure of Malcolm X in 1964, the movement established new mosques and increased the circulation of its weekly newspaper, *Muhammad Speaks.*

The NOI remained an annoyance, to say the least, to the liberal, pro-American view of Islam that many Sunni and Shiʻa Muslims, especially Arab American Muslims, continued to promulgate in the United States. There was fascination with and simultaneous repulsion felt by several leaders with the Nation of Islam's unorthodox teachings about Islam, which included a belief in the divinity of Nation of Islam founder W. D. Fard and the prophecy of the Messenger from Georgia, Elijah Muhammad. Foreign leaders such as Gamal Abdel Nasser and some American Muslim leaders such as Muhammad Abdul-Rauf were interested in cultivating ties to and making alliances with the Nation of Islam. But for many local leaders of Muslim congregations, including African American leaders of Ahmadi and Sunni congregations, the success of the Nation of Islam as perhaps the best organized, the best funded, and the most popular Muslim organization in the United States was frustrating, even maddening at times. The same was true for American-born and foreign-born missionaries who were associated with the South Asian–based Tablighi Jama'at, the Egyptian-based Muslim Brothers, and the Saudi-funded Muslim World League, established in 1961. The Nation of Islam accounted for almost half of all operating Muslim congregations in the United States, and its budget, though secret, was likely in the millions of dollars by the 1960s. Upon Elijah Muhammad's death in 1975, he was estimated to be worth tens of millions. *Muhammad Speaks* had a circulation in the tens of thousands, if not the hundreds of thousands—making it one of the most read Black newspapers in the country. Beginning in the 1960s, the Nation of Islam's competitors had launched a variety of attacks against the legitimacy of Elijah Muhammad and the group itself. The intellectual machinery of the Nation of Islam responded with a vigorous defense of the Messenger's Islamic authenticity while also seeking through aggressive street recruiting to maintain a rate of congregational growth that most Muslim American organizations could only envy.[24]

The strong institutional presence of the Nation of Islam translated into a threat to the hegemony of modern, reformist, and ultimately liberal visions of Islam. Its very structure, a Muslim organization based not so much on authoritative readings of the Qur'an and the Sunna as on the prophetic authority of a man from Georgia who lacked formal education, Arabic literacy, and traditional Islamic credentials, was revolutionary. It created a new source of mystical, charismatic Islamic authority at a time in which Islamic reform and renewal groups such as the Muslim Brothers and the Jama'at-i Islami were challenging the legitimacy of such authority. Moreover, the Nation of Islam's interpretation of Islam as a religion of Black liberation contradicted the liberal notion, then ascendant, that Islam was a religion that eliminated racial prejudice. It is no wonder that liberals and even some leftists, Muslim or not, reacted apoplectically to the group's teaching. Figures ranging from the nineteenth-century Liberian nationalist Edward Wilmot Blyden and Indian Ahmadi missionary Muhammad Sadiq to historian Arnold Toynbee and Islamic Center of Geneva director Sa'id Ramadan were agreed: Islam was the most antiracist religion in the world.[25] The Nation of Islam concurred but went further, articulating an Islamic theology of Black chosenness that rejected the desirability of integration. Finally, the Nation of Islam's anti-American critique was undesirable to many doggedly anticommunist reformers. Instead, the Nation of Islam allied itself and its Islamic teachings with Third World revolutionaries and the nonaligned movement.[26]

The Liberal/Conservative Side of the NOI

Even as the Nation of Islam challenged a postwar liberal world order linked to US military power, Euro-American proxy wars in the Third World, white supremacy, and Christian identity, it also advocated and enforced conservative elements of American culture among its membership. In the 1950s and early 1960s, Elijah Muhammad's Victorian and heteronormative approach to human sexuality and gender relations did not distinguish his movement from many other religious groups, whether conservative or liberal. For example, until the late 1960s and the 1970s, it might be argued, the mainstream liberal position in American religious organizations on matters of women's reproductive rights was not very different from the conservative one. At the very least, the gap between liberal and conservative religionists widened as conservatives identified the 1973 *Roe v. Wade* decision, which effectively defined abortion as an individual right of women (during a certain period of time during pregnancy), as a key issue for the practice of Christianity and other religious traditions in the United States.[27]

Throughout this period, young and old leaders of the Nation of Islam remained committed to conservative notions of gender and sexuality. The official gender and sexual ethics of the Nation of Islam were derived from the prophetic pronouncements of Elijah Muhammad, but they were also informed by a much older politics of respectability. Popular in Elijah Muhammad's youth, Victorian constructions of the Black body responded to the physical and emotional harm that Black people in the United States faced during the so-called nadir in race relations from 1880 to 1920. Black religious thought often sought to protect the Black body from lynching and job discrimination by making it "respectable." Also called "civilizationism," this important aspect of African American religious and secular culture emphasized the need for the Black body to be morally clean, pure, strong, well-dressed, disciplined, chaste, and industrious. Men and women had distinctly different roles in the ethical system that was anchored in these bourgeois assumptions. Appropriating these old values under a new religious teaching called Islam, Elijah Muhammad managed to reinterpret such ethics for his followers. Clothing these ethics as an embodied component of Islamic religion was itself transgressive because such a signification undermined the US nationalist and Christian identity to which middle-class Black respectability aspired.[28] But it was also conservative. As Darlene Clark Hine points out more generally of Afrocentrism, it "blurs easy distinctions between conservative and radical because it fosters liberation *and* fuels essentialism, empowers people *and* polices boundaries."[29]

Both in oral history interviews reflecting back on the late 1960s and the early 1970s and in documents from the time, hundreds of women went on record to say that they liked the conservative ethics of the movement. At the same time that many second-wave feminists criticized the movement as horribly sexist, these women praised the group's

Islamic ethos. Some wanted brother members to protect them from violence. Others sometimes referred to themselves as "queens" and wrote poems praising the head scarves and flowing gowns that adorned their royal bodies. Some female members asked rhetorically, What's wrong with a brother opening a door for a lady? Male members often made sure that women got home safely from organization meetings, and in some places the threat of male retribution deterred potential sexual and physical abuse. In addition, many women praised how men in the Nation of Islam were held to a high moral standard. Those who had sex outside marriage were put on trial and shunned. Men were also required to give up alcoholic beverages and were told that they had the responsibility to support their families financially. White women were often depicted as temptresses in official Nation of Islam literature—and Malcolm X, who had once dated white women, alluded to Black male desire for white female partners as a form of psychosis. These aspects of Elijah Muhammad's ethics were cited favorably by many Black women in the movement. For many female members, such conservative values, when enacted by the men in their lives, often felt liberating.[30]

At the same time, men and women in the movement challenged or subverted some of the conservative rules they found oppressive. For young male jazz fans in the Nation of Islam, the prohibition against intoxicants did not always apply to the use of marijuana in spaces outside the gaze of local movement leaders. Elijah Muhammad's condemnation of musical performance in the mosque was often ignored, as various mosques had de facto jazz groups and hosted concerts. By the late 1960s, many younger men and women in the movement were also experimenting with Afrocentric styles of dress, prompting Elijah Muhammad to issue a stern warning to Muslim women wearing dashikis and jejes.[31]

In addition, some women ignored the prohibition against the use of birth control. Tubal ligations and birth control pills were both seen by movement leadership as existential threats to the Black race. Such fears were not irrational. State medical authorities still sterilized significant numbers of Black, poor, and disabled women without their consent into the 1970s. Like other Black activists of the time, Elijah Muhammad saw the spread of widely available birth control as potential racial genocide. Since unmarried men and women in the movement were not supposed to have sex outside of wedlock in any case, various columnists for the movement newspaper instead offered advice on how to control and channel sexual desire into spiritual activities. If the unmarried member was unsuccessful in so doing and he or she was caught fornicating, prosecution and shunning would result. Married women were expected to be sexually active with their husbands, but they often used some form of birth control to control the size of their families. Some women said that using birth control was a matter of life and death, that their physicians advised them that having additional children could be dangerous to their health. Women made such decisions on a case-by-case basis. Thus, the conservative edicts of their prophet were reinterpreted, transformed, or violated in daily life.[32]

Gender and sexuality were not the only areas of movement activity that contained such contradictions or complexity. The use of the US legal system to defend the individual rights of members was yet another strategy that contained both liberal and radical elements. The refusal of movement members to be inducted into the US armed forces was radical in that it explicitly challenged US patriotism and the social contract of US citizenship. But when it came time to defend members in the courts, movement lawyers made First Amendment claims that their clients were simply practicing freedom of religion. In the case of Muhammad Ali, the argument was that since his religion prohibited participation in offensive war, he should be granted conscientious objector (CO) status. It is worth noting here that the religion to which the lawyers were referring was not Sunni Islam, but the interpretation of Islam revealed by the Messenger Elijah Muhammad—an interpretation of Islam that allowed for only personal self-defense. Members' claim to CO status was reasonable, though it was ultimately denied in Ali's case. Ali won his case on appeal in 1971, but the US Supreme Court ruled on technical grounds, avoiding the larger issue of whether Ali was entitled to CO status.[33]

The use of the US state and federal courts to protect the individual rights of Nation of Islam members was not isolated. In fact, from the perspective of US legal history, the far more consequential use of the courts in this manner was in the area of prisoners' rights. Muslim prisoners wished to gather for religious meetings, read religious literature, receive visits from Muslim ministers (which is what they were called in the Nation of Islam), eat pork-free food, and celebrate religious holidays such as Ramadan (which was celebrated in the Nation of Islam during Advent rather than during the Islamic month of Ramadan). Unlike *Clay v. United States*, the Supreme Court case that threw out Ali's conviction, some of these rulings set precedent, thus influencing the history of US jurisprudence with regard to all prisoners. Among the precedent-setting cases involving members of the Nation of Islam was *Fulwood v. Clemmer*, a case decided by the US District Court for the District of Columbia in 1962, which ruled that prisoners had the right to wear religious medals and attend religious services. That same year, the New York State Court of Appeals said in *Brown v. McGinnis* that members of the Nation of Islam had the right to sue for their religious liberty in state courts. Finally, and most importantly, in 1964 the US Supreme Court ruled in *Cooper v. Pate* that members of the Nation of Islam had "standing" to sue prison officials in federal courts for religious discrimination. The ruling came as a blow not only to prison officials who hoped to effectively ban the Nation of Islam but also to law enforcements agencies, especially the FBI, which had been arguing since the 1950s that the Nation of Islam was a political movement, not a legitimate religion. This was also the argument of the State of Illinois, which lost the case. This precedent thus limited, for a time, the use of the courts by federal and state officials to retard the growth of the Nation of Islam. After those rulings, the movement would have to be considered a legal religious organization in any US litigation.[34]

While such victories by the Nation of Islam increased their standing in the eyes of the law and also among liberals outside the movement, the group's reliance on the discourse of individual rights seemed to capitulate to the very nation from which they were seeking a separate identity. Even as the NOI was struggling against white supremacy and for Black empowerment, the use of the courts represented a form of assimilation. Relying on the US legal system lent legitimacy to the state and, perhaps most importantly, led Nation of Islam members to rehearse the social contract of liberalism at the heart of US nationalism. By the 1970s, some Nation of Islam members under the new leadership of W. D. Mohammed would become flag-waving US patriots, and one wonders if the habituation of organization members in the 1960s into the legal promise of liberalism did not in fact prepare the political ground for the sudden appearance of US nationalism among people who had been dissenters in the 1960s. Perhaps, however, the use of the courts was ultimately cynical, a tactic appropriated not out of devotion to the individual rights tradition but as a means to strengthen their organization and protect its members from harm.

Though the Nation of Islam's interaction with the US legal system can be interpreted in a variety of ways, one area of its ideology and practice seemed unambiguously, even classically liberal—namely, its belief in free markets and the encouragement of Black capitalism. This, too, was a form of assimilation in that the movement became complicit in an economic system that put African Americans at a competitive disadvantage. Elijah Muhammad taught that thrift, industriousness, capital investment and accumulation, and punctuality—in short, the values of modern industrial capitalism—were part of Islam. Professionals such as dentist Leo McCallum were lauded for their knowledge and success, while working-class members often aspired to become small business owners. The social networks of members in each city created both a consumer market and an internal sales force for various goods, and the movement became known for its entrepreneurial spirit. Decades after the heyday of the Nation of Islam, the organization is remembered across urban America for its sales of the bean pie—which allowed women in the Nation of Islam to supplement family incomes by baking pies in their home kitchens and then selling them in or immediately outside the mosque or asking their male relatives to do so on various street corners. In addition, members of the Nation of Islam established bakeries, restaurants, barbershops, and other small stores, often in the same neighborhood or street on which the mosque was located. Before they achieved success as small business owners or managers, younger men in the movement often spent time selling their quotas of the *Muhammad Speaks* newspaper, becoming known in Black neighborhoods and along busy streets for their aggressive but polite salesmanship.[35]

In addition to serving as a small business incubator, the Nation of Islam itself became big business. Or, more accurately, Elijah Muhammad became a big businessman. By the early 1970s, he owned a small bank, a dairy, a meat processing plant, and farms in Georgia, Michigan, and Alabama. In 1974, the year before his death, he also launched a fish import business, Whiting H&G (headed and gutted). All of these businesses benefited from the internal markets and built-in sales force for their goods. The fish could be sold by the same young men who hawked the newspaper. Movement members and the general public were encouraged to purchase their groceries and baked goods from Muslim-owned stores that were supplied by Elijah Muhammad's farms, dairy, and meat processing plant.

The focus on foodstuffs in this vertically integrated, multimillion-dollar business reflected Elijah Muhammad's ethical teachings about the Black body, which meant that the religious ecosystem of the movement embodied an emphasis on bodily purity, patriarchy, and productivity. The prophetic pronouncements that commanded members to practice values of sexual discipline, healthy eating, good hygiene, and respectable dress were joined by demands that one become economically productive, whether at home or in the marketplace. So, in addition to studying the lessons of their prophet, attending temple meetings, and fishing for new members, Nation of Islam families sought to exhibit their commitment to Islam through market-oriented activity. In Elijah Muhammad's view, this productivity and capital accumulation was supposed to lead to some degree of self-determination in a white-dominated marketplace.

Elijah Muhammad did not critique the techniques and rules of capitalism so much as he sought to get his own piece of the pie. In so doing,
he replicated the capitalist ideologies of past leaders such as Booker T.
Washington and Marcus Garvey, who framed Black liberation at least
partially in terms of Black capitalism. As with the Nation of Islam's
use of the US legal system, the advocacy of entrepreneurial and petit-
bourgeois economic activity no doubt aided some individual members
of the organization and stood as a psychological and symbolic victory
over ideas of Black inferiority and generational poverty.[36]

But the NOI did little to change the American version of economic
liberalism that put African Americans at a competitive disadvantage.
Though the organization called for the establishment of a separate
Black nation funded by the US government, it offered little in the way
of organizing and agitating to achieve such a lofty goal. Focused on
small business and personal thrift, the movement's "do for self" philosophy could not offer a realistic, structural solution to the problem
of the wealth gap between Black and non-Black Americans. Postwar
American liberalism's emphasis on equal rights and state welfare was
not enough to correct this gap either. In reality, the legal equality advocated by liberals made the problem of economic inequality worse
because white Americans entered the competition for resources and
status with far more economic and political capital than African Americans did. As a group, whites had been able to take advantage of better educational and employment opportunities, federal funding for
housing, and looking further back in US history, massive government
handouts like the 1862 Homestead Act, which gave 160-acre land tracts
formerly occupied by Native Americans in the West to white settlers.
Having accumulated far more wealth than Black people, most of whose
families had been enslaved until the 1860s and then Jim Crowed until
the 1960s, middle- and upper-class white people could afford to live in
"better" school districts, to send their kids to college, to give their children money for house down payments, to borrow money at lower interest rates, to purchase vehicles and other goods at lower prices, and to

leave money to family members in their wills. The legal desegregation of schools and federal guarantees of nondiscrimination in employment and housing were supposed to put African Americans on an equal footing to white people, and they did result in some improvement, but legal equality did not fix the problem of white privilege.[37] After more than fifty years of legal equality, in 2016 white families in the United States had a median net worth of $171,100 while Black families had a median net worth of $17,600.[38] The liberal dream of racial equality had failed African Americans.

Elijah Muhammad may have been prophetic indeed in preaching that only the apocalypse would deliver Black people from such injustice. The NOI leader taught that at the end of the current dispensation of world history a Mothership would appear in the sky and destroy white people, or more precisely, the whiteness in the human race. Blacks, the original humans, would become the rulers of the planet, a position they had once held when the Tribe of Shabazz ruled the Holy City of Mecca. Until then, the Messenger taught, Muslims should reform themselves morally, separate from whites, and work for economic success. While such teachings may have helped to redirect any impulses for political or economic revolution among members of the movement, they did not stand in the way of the movement's focus on worldly success. Elijah Muhammad told his followers to live their lives in the here and now rather than to wait for the sweet by-and-by. Heaven and hell, he preached, were states of mind on earth, not separate worlds to which one goes after death.[39]

By the late 1960s, these teachings came under fire from many younger activists in the Black Power movement for their lack of revolutionary ideology and action. While groups such as the Black Panther Party clearly built on the notions of Black identity that the Nation of Islam had popularized, many of their members expressed the same frustration with the organization that Malcolm X had felt during the early 1960s. Critiques of the Nation of Islam did not focus on its radical symbolic protest of white supremacy, US nationalism, US foreign policy, or Christianity—in fact, those critiques would be adopted and adapted by an increasing number of African Americans—but rather on the nonviolent, insular, and politically quietistic nature of the movement.[40]

These critiques of the movement help to identify the shifting political ground on which this Muslim American group stood, fairly immovable, for decades. The movement's teachings, regarded by large numbers of both Black and white Americans as a radical assault on the ideological foundations of American culture during the era of the liberal consensus in the 1950s and 1960s, seemed politically quietistic or insufficiently "Black" by the 1970s. The movement also began to look different to some of the same liberals who in the early 1960s saw it as a threat to the promise of civil rights. When Elijah Muhammad died in 1975, for example, a *New York Times* editorial praised the leader for his ability to reform the lives of those whom federal programs had been unable to help and for his contributions to the Black pride movement.[41] By the 1970s, when Alex Haley's *Roots* became a national bestseller, it seems that even the stark Black separatism of the Nation of Islam could be viewed as yet another form of ethnic revival and heritage.[42]

The changing ways in which the Nation of Islam was viewed, and by whom, offer helpful indices by which the evolving meaning of liberalism in the United States during the twentieth century can be evaluated. The Nation of Islam was regarded as so countercultural that it exposed the nature of what historian Arthur Schlesinger Jr. had dubbed the "vital center," that is, the liberal Western alternative to communism and socialism. Seen as seditious by the FBI during World War II and prosecuted as such, the Nation of Islam became merely subversive, but even more dangerous, to law enforcement agencies by the 1950s and 1960s. Though law-abiding and largely nonviolent, the Nation of Islam encouraged a moral and political geography among Black Americans that denied the legitimacy of claims by both the nation-state and the Christian church to the loyalty of African Americans. In the United States, Black liberals were as likely as white liberals to condemn the racial separatism of the movement, which was viewed as a threat to and negation of the dream of a racially integrated society. Foreign Muslim students and many domestic Muslims outside the Nation of Islam criticized the movement as religiously illegitimate. But beyond the borders of the United States, Third World revolutionary leaders, including Muslims in Africa and Asia, came to see the Nation of Islam, especially in the persons of Malcolm X and Muhammad Ali, as a potential ally in their attempts to throw off a colonized consciousness and oppose US foreign policy in their countries and regions.

While this aspect of Nation of Islam politics remained a radical component of the movement under the leadership of Elijah Muhammad and later Louis Farrakhan, other aspects of the movement increasingly came to be seen as conservative by both Black liberals and radicals in the 1970s. The emphasis on Victorian gender relations was sometimes framed as reactionary, while the endorsement of Islam over African traditional religion was sometimes labeled a form of Black self-hatred. For Black socialists, it goes without saying that the Nation of Islam's enthusiastic endorsement of capital accumulation and petit-bourgeois behaviors was anathema. Strangely enough, by the 1970s many American liberals had found something in the movement to respect. The fact that its one-time critics had become at least partial admirers shows how much US politics, both liberal and conservative, had begun to change. In the aftermath of Vietnam and the Watergate scandal, the Nation of Islam's essential distrust of the US government was widely shared by US citizens. More and more people in the mainstream saw their government as hypocritical and became cynical about its prosecution of dissenters. The Nation of Islam may not have been liked much more, but it no longer seemed so dangerous.

But the NOI's legacy as a national voice of political dissent in the 1950s and 1960s continues to offer a helpful analytic for understanding the dominant form of American liberalism that is tied to racism and US imperialism. The problems that it identified—namely, the racialized nature of inequality and its connections to US militarism abroad—still characterize US politics in the twenty-first century. As critics pointed out, however, the movement's conservative side meant that, in practice, the movement also reified the very social structures of capitalist, liberal hegemony. This was one of the reasons why, as the next chapter shows, Malcolm X left the movement and articulated a more full-throated revolutionary Muslim American political vision that sought the end of white cultural, political, and economic supremacy.

3

Malcolm X and the Islamic Politics of Global Black Liberation

As Malcolm X prepared to address the Young Men's Muslim Association (YMMA) in Cairo, Egypt, on July 27, 1964, he jotted down an outline of the speech in his travel diary. In Cairo to attend the summit of the Organization of African Unity just days before, the former Nation of Islam minister and now head of the Muslim Mosque, Inc., in Harlem, New York, had stayed in Egypt to undergo training as a Muslim missionary. The speech gave Malcolm X an opportunity to cement his burgeoning partnership with the Egyptian government's Supreme Council of Islamic Affairs, which sponsored his months-long residency in the country. It was also a chance to seek the moral, political, and financial support of a foreign Muslim audience for the African American liberation struggle. The figure of Egyptian president and Third World hero Gamal Abdel Nasser loomed large in the outline of the speech not only as a political revolutionary but also as an embodiment of Islamic ethics. In his notes, Malcolm X listed nine different points about Nasser:

1. Your President is my President
2. A Man: fearless, far-reaching (wise)
3. Uncompromising on the side of freedom
4. Supports (always) African Freedom Fighters
5. Supports freedom everywhere

1. Brought freedom to Egypt (Africa)
2. [R]eturned the Suez to Africans
3. Defeated the foreign invaders
4. Good man, good Muslim—may God bless him[1]

These comments were rhetorical gestures of praise and thanks tailored for his hosts and their leader, but they also reflected his thinking about how Nasser exemplified the religious and political identities to which Malcolm X himself ascribed. Nasser was a good Muslim, according to Malcolm X, but he was more than that. The list alluded to Nasser's accomplishments and his status as a global leader of a Pan-African, pro–Third World revolutionary politics that was nonaligned, that is, which sought to advance the national interests, sovereignty, and self-determination of newly independent states in the developing world rather than be used as pawns in the Cold War between the United States and the Soviet Union. In Nasser's 1955 book, *Egypt's Liberation: The Philosophy of the Revolution*, he argued that Egypt's identity resided in "three circles" of influence: the Arab, the African, and the Islamic.[2] Nasser sought to be a leader in all three spheres, though he emerged from the 1956 Suez Crisis (in which he successfully weathered and faced down the invasion of Israeli, British, and French troops) as a star of the Afro-Asian nonaligned movement as well.

By drawing on underutilized correspondence and diaries from 1964, we are able to see how Malcolm X constructed an Islamic ethics of liberation inspired by Nasser's example.[3] This chapter demonstrates how he offered a more direct, more revolutionary challenge than the Nation of Islam to postwar American liberalism and the assimilation of Muslims to anti-Black racism and US colonialism. It contests the conventional view that Malcolm X's 1964 hajj, or pilgrimage to Mecca, was the ultimate symbol of his spiritual journey from street hustler to Nation of Islam minister and finally Sunni Muslim believer. Such mythologizing often turns Malcolm X into a liberal saint of interracial cooperation. But Mecca was not the real center of Malcolm X's newfound identity as a Sunni Muslim. Cairo was. For Malcolm X, Cairo represented what he described as a "progressive" response to American liberalism. For him, the Islamic socialism and Afro-Asian solidarity of Gamal Abdel Nasser's Egypt rather than the monarchical, conservative ideology of Nasser's Saudi Arabian rivals represented the heart of Islamic religion and the key to the liberation of all people of color. Malcolm X's Islamic ethics of global Black liberation was not a detailed political platform; it was a moral argument that the Muslim world had a religious obligation to fight for the freedom of all people of color, whether Muslim or not.

Malcolm was a critic of American democracy and he pointed out its critical flaws. He believed that radical change was needed and he sought allies to end white supremacy both at home and abroad. But there was little room for such dissent in 1960s America. American liberalism was not "liberal" enough to accommodate Malcolm X because he called out liberalism's reliance on racism and imperialism. As with the Nation of Islam, the US government identified him as a national security threat and his citizenship rights were cast aside. Malcolm X refused to accept that second-class status and he saw Islam as a resource that inspired a different kind of life for Black people.

I build on Manning Marable's suggestive assertion that at the end of Malcolm X's life, Islam became "the spiritual platform from which he constructed a politics of Third World revolution."[4] In the revolutionary leader's thinking, however, Islam was more than a spiritual system; indeed, he spoke and wrote only a little about the sacred, the soul, or other typically spiritual matters. For him, the heart of Islam, and of religion more generally, was ethics, which for him meant the ways in which human beings ought to behave not only in private and individual matters but also in public affairs—that is, in political life. This understanding of ethics was consonant with the Social Gospel tradition of American Christianity and more particularly with the prophetic tradition of African American religion that informed many twentieth-century African American religious movements.[5]

Malcolm X's linking of Islam to the freedom of the so-called Dark World also represented a continuation of a religious and political philosophy that he first articulated as a leader in Elijah Muhammad's Nation of Islam. Like many other African American radicals in the Cold War era, he reimagined the domestic civil rights movement as an international struggle for human rights and political self-determination. Many historians have shown how he sought alliances and argued for greater cooperation with various government officials, activists, and intellectuals from Africa, the Middle East, and the Muslim world.[6] Once formally separated from the organization in early 1964, Malcolm X continued to argue for the idea that Islam was, at its very core, a religious and political system of liberation from white oppression. But instead of citing the prophetic utterances of Elijah Muhammad as proof of Islam's revolutionary ethics, he began to appeal to other sources of religious authority, specifically the Sunni Islamic tradition, in arguing that the liberation of socially, economically, and politically disenfranchised Muslim and non-Muslim people, especially people of color in both the United States and abroad, was a moral obligation for all practicing Muslims. He was not content to wait on the Mothership to destroy white supremacy—which is how Elijah Muhammad prophesied that the white-dominated world would end.[7] Instead, he would seek the help of Africans, Muslims, and others to liberate African Americans as part of a broader global struggle. And at times, he would even appeal to liberal ideals and liberal institutions in order to advance his goal of Black liberation.

Looking past both the bipolar struggle between the Soviet Union and the United States and the politics of African American liberalism, Malcolm X identified nonaligned political allies as necessary to the struggle against white supremacy both at home and abroad. This is why it was so important for him to develop close ties with those government officials and power brokers in the developing world who possessed the clout and financial resources to wage a campaign on behalf of all people of color. As his visits to newly independent sub-Saharan African states demonstrate, these players included leaders such as Kenyan prime minister and subsequent president Jomo Kenyatta, Ghanaian president Kwame Nkrumah, and Ugandan prime minister Milton Obote. But just as important to Shabazz's goals were the governments of the United Arab Republic (UAR) and Saudi Arabia.

During 1964, Malcolm X spent five months abroad, mostly in Egypt and Saudi Arabia.[8] During this time, he performed the pilgrimage to

Mecca and took on a new name, El-Hajj Malik El-Shabazz. Though he would continue to answer to the name Malcolm X in the United States, many of his Muslim brothers and sisters both at home and abroad were proud to call him "El-Hajj," the pilgrim, and often used his new name. During his travels, Malcolm X/Malik Shabazz embraced, challenged, adapted, and negotiated the many new ideas that he encountered.[9] As part of their public diplomacy, Saudi and Egyptian missionaries, religious functionaries, and government officials sought to make Shabazz an ally; his dairies and correspondence from this period illustrate that he was highly strategic in his dealings with them. Declaring at one point that "my heart is in Cairo," Shabazz identified Nasserism as a form of Islam that tied religion to revolution. But he pursued the financial support and religious imprimatur of the anti-Nasserite and Saudi-funded Muslim World League as well. Shabazz desired their support in order to buoy the culture of Islamic learning, the knowledge of Islamic rituals, the study of the Qur'an, and other pietistic practices among his African American Muslim followers. Though he saw the Saudis as too conservative and he viewed their sometime allies, the Egyptian Muslim Brothers, as tone deaf to anti-Black racism, Shabazz identified in their Islamic missionary activities and their emphasis on the need for a genuine religious revival the potential to ignite political action that would challenge the anti-Black racism and US militarism abroad that were part and parcel of American liberalism.

The Nation of Islam: Malcolm X's Road to Cairo

To understand how Shabazz came to embrace an Islamic ethics of liberation that offered a critique of American liberalism, anti-Black racism, and US military intervention abroad, it is necessary to trace the formation of his religious and political consciousness in the Nation of Islam.[10] The Nation of Islam was no detour on Shabazz's road to Cairo; it was the place where Shabazz first linked Black liberation to Islamic religion. For Malcolm X, who served as minister of the Nation of Islam's Temple

No. 7 in Harlem in the 1950s, the nonaligned movement of Third World countries against both Soviet and US interference in their foreign and domestic policies became a sign of changing political winds. The 1955 Afro-Asian Conference in Bandung, Indonesia, was a signal event. "O, dark nations, of the East, know this," he proclaimed in a sermon made sometime in 1955 or early 1956, "there are over seventeen million of us here in America who are being awakened by the Honorable Elijah Muhammad. Though we have long been 'dead,' we know today that we are your long lost brothers."[11] As the chief spokesperson for the movement's prophetic leader, Elijah Muhammad, Malcolm X drew out the radical elements of its theology and doctrine, fusing them with Third World nonalignment. He positioned the organization as the US vanguard of the global movement not only to eschew colonial and neo-colonial political control but also to rid people of color of a colonized consciousness.[12] In so doing, Shabazz identified Gamal Abdel Nasser as a model of anticolonial, Afro-Asian Islamic leadership. He was not the only African American leader to do so. Fellow Harlemite street orator Carlos Cooks called Nasser a "unique and rare personality," both "African and Arabic."[13] Seen in light of the Montgomery Bus Boycott of 1955 and 1956, Nasser's rhetoric and leadership through the Suez Crisis in 1956 struck many African Americans as a model of strength and persistence.[14] In 1956, Israel, Great Britain, and France invaded Egypt, but the Soviet Union and the United States demanded that they withdraw. Nasser emerged a victor in the crisis and he became a hero to many African American political radicals.[15]

In New York, Malik Shabazz was part of this world, where he developed an informal intellectual, social, and political network of Africans and African Americans, foreign and domestic Muslims, and other figures committed to the solidarity of the Dark World.[16] One pivotal member of this network was the Christian minister and Harlem Congressman Adam Clayton Powell Jr., who had attended the Afro-Asian Conference in Bandung. When Powell invited Indonesian officials to visit Harlem in July 1957, Shabazz was on hand to greet them. On this occasion, he praised Powell's support of the Indonesians' visit. "The 90 million Moslems in Indonesia," Shabazz said at a public event with the visitors, "are only a small part of the 600 million more in other parts of the Dark World." During the same period, Shabazz also hosted various Muslim diplomats from the United Nations, including Syrian ambassador Rafik Asha and Egyptian attaché Ahmad Zaki al-Borai at a Temple No. 7 celebration.[17]

In 1958, Malcolm X's fame and his connections to a growing number of Africans and Muslims led to an invitation from Egyptian officials to visit the Middle East. He made the visit the following year. Acting as Elijah Muhammad's emissary, he was to pave the way for his leader's visit to Egypt and then Saudi Arabia, where, later in 1959, Elijah Muhammad performed an *'umra*, or out-of-season pilgrimage to Mecca—and then visited Pakistan. Al-Borai accompanied Shabazz to the airport on July 5, and, once in Egypt, Shabazz met with Anwar al-Sadat, Nasser's two-time vice president, in addition to visiting officials from Egypt's Al-Azhar University. It is unclear exactly what was said during these meetings, but Malcolm X later admitted to Pakistani American entrepreneur and Nation of Islam supporter Abdul Basit Naeem that when it came time to perform the prescribed prayers (*salat*), he was only able to mumble along and imitate what others were doing. From Cairo, where a case of diarrhea scuttled at least some of his planned activities, Shabazz briefly visited Khartoum, Jerusalem, Damascus, and, finally, Jidda, Saudi Arabia. He arrived back in New York by July 22.[18]

Malcolm X gave glowing reports to fellow Nation of Islam members and showed them films from his visit upon his return. He told them that "the Muslims in Egypt and Africa" were blacker than he was.[19] His letters from both Jidda and Khartoum were also published in the *Pittsburgh Courier*, the African American newspaper that first carried Elijah Muhammad's columns in the 1950s and often featured news about Africa and the Third World more generally. Writing for a domestic Black American audience, Malcolm X depicted the people of Arabia as racial brothers and sisters—their "facial appearance" and "regal black and rich brown" color would make them feel right "at home in Harlem," he opined. Noting that "99 percent" of people in Jidda would be "jim-crowed" in the United States, he argued that the lack of color preju-dice in Arabia was due to the Islamic principle of racial equality. While Christianity made the same rhetorical claims to racial equality, he wrote, it was an actual "way of life" in Islam.[20]

Why would Malcolm X assert that Arabs were people of color and paint such a romantic view of racial harmony in the Arab world? To be sure, his framing of race in the Arab world was at least in part a response to widespread criticisms in the African American press of Saudi Ara-bia, which did not outlaw slavery until 1962.[21] But Sudan and Sudanese Muslims played just as important a role in the leader's optimistic fram-ing of race in the Arab world. In Sudan, Malcolm X's host was educator and Islamic activist Malik Badri, who toured him around both Khar-toum and nearby Omdurman, cities where Malcolm X encountered the Arabic-speaking Black African culture about which Elijah Muhammad had been preaching, in a mythological register, for decades. Badri took him to schools and markets, and feted him as an honored guest in his brother's home.[22] Sudan was an example for Malcolm X of a country in which Black, Muslim, and Arabic-speaking identities were complemen-tary, not contradictory.

During this 1959 trip, Malcolm X also observed that many Black Mus-lims had achieved a social status in the Arab world unimaginable in the United States at the time. Egyptian vice president Anwar Sadat, for ex-ample, was the son of a Sudanese mother and, despite being ridiculed by some fellow Egyptians as Nasser's "black poodle," still eventually became president. By the 1960s, Malcolm X publicly acknowledged the presence of anti-Black racism in the Middle East, but he repeated pan-Islamist Abd al-Rahman Azzam's argument that "the problems of color which exist in the Muslim world exist only where, and to what extent that . . . area of the Muslim world has been influenced by the West."[23] What-ever doubts Malcolm X may have held about racial equality in the Arab world in the late 1950s and the 1960s, such thoughts were not going to interfere with his larger goal of linking the domestic struggle of African Americans to the Afro-Asian struggle against neocolonialism. It was too important to convince African Americans that their destinies lay with not with the promises of Cold War Black liberals but instead with their more natural Black and brown allies in Africa and Asia.[24]

This vision was also, according to Malcolm X, part of God's will. When he addressed Adam Clayton Powell's Abyssinian Baptist Church in June 1963, he framed the Black revolution as "part of God's divine plan," arguing that God "will not rest until he has used his religion to establish one world—a universal, one-world brotherhood."[25] Malcolm X's understanding that the teleological goals of Islam were the same as the political goals of the Black revolution was an expression of the Nation of Islam's larger view of both religion and politics. Implicitly rejecting any secular notion that religion was a private individual set of beliefs while politics was the public expression of communal and shared goals, Elijah Muhammad, Malcolm X, and other intellectuals in the NOI interpreted Islam as both inherently religious and political. If religion did not contribute to the liberation of Black people from racist oppression, then it was not true religion but instead part of the system of oppression. According to the Nation of Islam, true religion—the religion of Islam—was by definition a religion of liberation.[26] Though Malcolm X later rejected Elijah Muhammad's prophecy as a legitimate source of Islamic authority, he maintained his belief that Islamic religion required social and political action.

As Malcolm X's celebrity (or, from the point of view of the FBI, notoriety) continued to grow in the late 1950s and early 1960s, more and more critics challenged his defense of Elijah Muhammad's doctrines. Rather than push them away, Malcolm X developed close, if also contested relationships with some of these people. "Long before Malcolm could come to Mecca," writes biographer Louis A. DeCaro Jr., "Mecca seemed to have come to Malcolm."[27] During this era, foreign and American-born Muslim students at US universities were organizing campus ministries, and Sunni Muslim-sponsored groups from the Middle East were beginning to develop *da'wa*, or missionizing, as an organized activity in non-Muslim lands.[28] These groups reached out to Malcolm X, who was arguably the most articulate and powerful Muslim spokesperson in the United States at the time.[29] Sunni Muslim students and the representatives or allies of missionary groups approached him as he toured college campuses. He also debated many Muslim critics of the Nation of Islam in New York City. Writing letters to the editor of newspapers such as the *Amsterdam News* and the *New York Times*, Malcolm X answered Elijah Muhammad's naysayers, defending the prophetic leader's religious and political philosophy of racial separatism against attacks by Sunni Muslim students and other practitioners.[30]

But he also carefully considered their arguments. For example, when Ahmed Osman, a Dartmouth student of Sudanese heritage, sought him out at Harlem's Mosque No. 7 in 1962 to challenge him on the legitimacy of Elijah Muhammad's teachings, Malcolm X agreed to read the Sunni Muslim missionary literature that the student offered, stayed in touch with Osman, and asked for more. The literature that he read was from the Islamic Center in Geneva, Switzerland, a community run by Sa'id Ramadan, the son-in-law of Hassan al-Banna, founder of the Muslim Brothers in Egypt. The Muslim Brotherhood was Egypt's premier Islamist group, focusing on political and religious reform of Egyptian society and the state under the banner of Islamic religion.[31]

While it may be too much to attribute Malcolm X's changing attitudes toward Elijah Muhammad to the influence of Sunni Islamic teachings or Sunni Muslim organizations, it is clear that he began to alter his interpretations of Elijah Muhammad's teachings, including the idea that the white man was the devil, well before he formally separated from the group. "When you are a Muslim," he said on the Washington, DC, radio program *Focus*, aired on May 12, 1963, "you don't look at the color of a man's skin. . . . You look at the man and judge him according to his conscious behavior."[32] Muslims in America, he said, should practice this principle in the same way that Muslims abroad did, an argument that indicated a shift in Shabazz's religious geography away from the "wilderness of North America," the land where W. D. Fard, God Incarnate, appeared to the prophet Elijah Muhammad, and toward the *umma*, or the worldwide community of Muslims.[33] Though he may have left the Nation of Islam because he could no longer tolerate Elijah Muhammad's philandering or, perhaps more importantly, Elijah Muhammad's approach to civil rights and political philosophy of Black liberation— which Malcolm X found to be too passive—he was also embracing a form of Islam he considered to be more "orthodox," as he makes clear in both his diaries and his autobiography.[34]

From the Arab Cold War to an Islamic Liberation Ethic

According to several sources, including the *Autobiography of Malcolm X*, the relationship with Osman and other Muslims led Malcolm X to seek out Mahmoud Yousef Shawarbi, an Egyptian professor of Islamic studies who had visited the United States in the 1950s, served as a visiting faculty member at New York's Fordham University on a Fulbright Fellowship, and in January 1964 was appointed head of the Federation of Islamic Associations of United States and Canada, the largest Sunni Muslim American group at the time.[35] As illustrated above, the man who would also become known as El-Hajj Malik El-Shabazz already possessed a large network of Muslim allies and conversation partners from sub-Saharan Africa, Pakistan, and the Middle East, but, over the next year, Arabic-speaking Muslims—Sudanese, Egyptian, and Saudi— played a particularly significant role in Malcolm X/Malik Shabazz's thinking. Shawarbi was one of them. He encouraged Shabazz to make the hajj and, most importantly, introduced him to the well-heeled Saudis and Egyptians who could make it possible.[36] One of those people was Abd al-Rahman Azzam.

Azzam, an Egyptian diplomat, was the architect and first secretary-general of the Arab League from 1945 to 1952. For decades, Azzam Pasha, as he was called, had been a prominent Egyptian nationalist, but after Gamal Abdel Nasser rose to power in the 1952 revolution against the

Egyptian monarchy, Azzam lost favor with the regime.[37] He moved to Saudi Arabia and became a leading theorist of what is sometimes called political Islam or Islamism, the belief that Islam is both a religion and a state (but not necessarily a theocracy).[38] The idea that Islam offered resources for political action and governance was not new to Azzam; the Egyptian national identity that he had advocated was informed by recognition of Egypt's Islamic heritage.[39] But in his Saudi exile, he devoted an increasing amount of his work to forging transnational ties among Muslims committed to evangelizing on behalf of a utopian vision of an Islamic society. His most famous book, which Shawarbi gave to Shabazz, was entitled *The Eternal Message of Muhammad*. The book reiterates the calls of various modern Muslim reformers that Islam could and should be the animating force behind the modern nation-state. Islam was a religion, Azzam said, but it was also "a law, a way of life, a 'nation,' and a 'state.'"[40] According to Azzam, the ideal Islamic nation-state would be governed by reason rather than superstition, respect the diversity of its citizens, and encourage in its citizenry the love of charity, fairness, industriousness, mercy, and solidarity. While theocratic in some respect, the Islamic nation-state opposed dictatorship; the consent of the state's citizens was required for legitimacy. In this Islamic utopia, many of liberalism's best elements would be preserved, while its less desirable aspects, such as materialism, colonialism, and class struggle, would be eliminated.

Shabazz read Azzam's book on his way to the hajj on April 13, 1964, but Shawarbi had given him more than the book. He also shared the phone number of Muhammad, his son, who lived in Cairo, and the phone number of Azzam's son, Omar Azzam, who lived in Jidda, Saudi Arabia.[41] When Shabazz was detained by the hajj court to determine his bona fides as a Muslim, it was Omar Azzam who interceded with Saudi authorities on his behalf. The Azzams were connected to the Saudi monarchy through marriage: the son of Prince Faysal, de facto ruler of the kingdom, was married to Azzam Pasha's daughter. With such royal connections, it was only a matter of time before the hajj court allowed

Shabazz to participate in the hajj. And Abdul Aziz Majid, then Saudi deputy chief of protocol, offered Shabazz a chauffeured car during his visit. During his time in Jidda, Shabazz stayed in Azzam's suite at the Jidda Palace Hotel. After the hajj was over, Prince Faysal himself met with Shabazz to make sure that Shabazz's conversion to Sunni Islam was sincere and legitimate.[42]

As Shabazz's network of Arab Muslim government officials, missionaries, contacts, and friends began to multiply, he entered a social and political world deeply shaped by a conflict between Nasser's UAR and Saudi Arabia. As the United States and the Soviet Union sought allies in their global Cold War, various Arab states began to align with, challenge, or play Soviet and US interests against one another; they also had to negotiate the popular desire for Arab political unity and widespread sympathy for the plight of Palestinians, who became stateless in 1948.[43] By the late 1950s, a regional conflict formed between those aligned with the Arab socialism of Egyptian president Gamal Abdel Nasser—which became increasingly seen by the US government as part of the Soviet sphere of influence—and those powers, often allies of the United States, opposed to Nasser's expansive vision of Arab political unity. In 1958, after Syria and Egypt formally united under Nasser's presidency in the UAR, other states in the Arab Middle East became vulnerable to popular revolutions inspired by or allied with Nasser. Months after the founding of the UAR, the army overthrew the Hashemite monarchy in Iraq, and an uprising against Lebanese president Camille Chamoun was put down only with the assistance of the US military. By 1962, Nasser had committed ground troops to the Yemeni civil war that pitted the republican forces of Abdullah al-Sallah against those loyal to the imamate. Saudi Arabia, which shared a border with Yemen, supported the latter.[44]

Another front in this Arab Cold War was the battle for hearts and minds, and it is into this crucible that Malik Shabazz was thrust. Shabazz's royal treatment in Saudi Arabia and his long stay in Egypt indicate that both Saudis and Egyptians prized their burgeoning relationship with the man who was likely the best known African American Sunni

Muslim in the United States. Shabazz became a player in the public relations and soft diplomacy fronts of the Arab Cold War as both UAR- and Saudi-sponsored organizations sought to use Islamic missionizing to gain Muslim allies and influence non-Muslim public opinion abroad.[45]

Nasser's nationalization of state institutions also attempted to influence and control how Islamic religion was being interpreted, taught, and applied in Egyptian schools, courts, and government agencies. According to historian Reinhold Schulze, "The wave of nationalization in industry and finance, which started in 1961, as well as new attempts to revive land reform, established the framework for an Islamic interpretation of socialism."[46] Nasser made sure that his political program of Arab nationalism, socialism, Pan-Africanism, and Third World solidarity was legitimated in Islamic terms. Thus, in 1960, the UAR established the Supreme Council of Islamic Affairs (SCIA) and charged it with promoting what might be called "Islamic liberation socialism" in the developing world.[47] In 1961, Nasser effectively nationalized Al-Azhar University in Cairo, striking fear in the hearts of some Saudi leaders that the Arab world's most fabled Islamic university would now produce Islamic scholarship supporting Nasserism.

The Saudis responded by expediting a plan to establish their own Islamic university in Medina.[48] From this point forward, the Kingdom of Saudi Arabia would spend significant funds to develop Islamic missionary activity as a form of soft power and cultural diplomacy. Tracing their own political legitimacy to the Wahhabi religious reform movement and their status as the protectors of the holy places in Mecca and Medina, Saudi Arabia began to offer financial support and to build a missionary infrastructure that would bolster its claims to be a leader of *dar al-islam*, meaning "Islamdom" or the "House of Islam." In 1962, the same year that Nasser committed ground troops to the civil war in Yemen, the Saudi government allied with Islamist activists from Asia and Africa to create the Muslim World League (MWL). The timing was not a coincidence. At the MWL inaugural conference, speakers strongly opposed Nasser and his form of Arabism, offering pan-Islamic unity as a counter to the powerful Arab populist. The meeting featured a "who's who" of activists, those committed to a greater or lesser degree to the same ideas outlined in Azzam's *Eternal Message of Muhammad*. They included Abul Ala Mawdudi of Pakistan's Jama'at-i Islami, Pakistan's most powerful Islamist organization, and Sa'id Ramadan, son-in-law of the founder of the Egyptian Muslim Brothers, which had been forcefully repressed by Nasser.[49]

Simply put, Malik Shabazz worked with people allied to both the UAR and Saudi governments, and in his public pronouncements in the United States, he did not take sides in the conflict. But in his private correspondence and in speeches made in Egypt, Shabazz was more forthcoming. As these documents reveal, he favored Nasser's revolutionary approach to the problems of people of color. Even though Nasser's critics in the MWL accused the Egyptian leader of being un-Islamic, Shabazz did not see it that way. Instead, he saw Nasser as a leader who was willing and able to bring to life an Islamic liberation ethics.

Shabazz developed this idea most fully in the speeches that he made during his long stay in Egypt during the second half of 1964. A few months after performing the pilgrimage to Mecca, touring West Africa, and briefly taking care of business at home in New York, Shabazz returned to Egypt to attend the African Summit Conference of the Organization of African Unity (OAU) from July 17 through July 21. Shabazz's goal was to convince African leaders that "our problem is your problem"—that is, to link the domestic struggles of African Americans in the United States for dignity and self-determination to the struggle of African states and colonies for political and economic independence.[50] With nearly every African head of state in attendance, Shabazz pleaded in an eight-page memo for the OAU to internationalize the US civil rights struggle. He hoped that the African states would support bringing the case of African Americans to the United Nations.

Shabazz's idea to bring the problems of Black America before the United Nations indicates the extent to which, even as he sought a radical reordering of global power, Malik Shabazz also attempted to work within and thus legitimize some of the foundational ideas and structures of the postwar liberal order. By presenting anti-Black racism in the United States as a key issue in the international struggle for human rights, Shabazz adopted the liberal language articulated in the Universal Declaration of Human Rights passed by the United Nations in 1948.[51] As he pleaded with African and Muslim leaders to bring the US government to account before the UN General Assembly, he was in part "naturalizing the American-led postwar liberal order rather than arguing for fully revolutionizing it."[52] American liberals, especially Eleanor Roosevelt, played a pivotal role in the creation of the UN and John D. Rockefeller donated the eighteen acres that would become the UN headquarters in New York City.[53] Moreover, Shabazz was asking a global organization that exemplified the postwar liberal order to intervene in the domestic affairs of a sovereign nation to advance the liberty and freedom of its African American inhabitants.

Perhaps most importantly, Shabazz's bid to involve African and Muslim leaders was explicitly supported by other prominent Black leaders, including some liberals. On June 13, 1964, Shabazz went to actor Sidney Poitier's house in upstate New York to meet with "Whitney Young of the National Urban League, representatives of A. Philip Randolph and CORE [Congress of Racial Equality], [and] Benjamin Davis of the Communist Party." Also on hand were Poitier, actor Ruby Dee, actor Ossie Davis, and attorney Clarence Jones, who was authorized to speak for Martin Luther King Jr. According to Davis, Shabazz proposed "to bring the Negro question before the United Nations to internationalize the whole question and bring it before the whole world."[54] The group heartily supported the idea and asked him to obtain support from the African and Middle Eastern leaders with whom he would be meeting in the second half of 1964. As Manning Marable documents, this is exactly what Shabazz did.[55]

During his long stay in Egypt after the OAU conference, it became clear that Shabazz remained committed not only to using liberal ideology to support the liberation of Black people but also to showing how human rights were consonant with Islamic religious values. After the conference, Shabazz underwent Islamic studies training from the SCIA, which welcomed the chance to host Shabazz and was willing to underwrite his travels.[56] According to Shabazz's diaries, Shawarbi continued to act as a main interlocutor with the Egyptian government and often with Egyptians more generally, though Shabazz also met and socialized with some Americans in Cairo, including *Egyptian Gazette* editor David DuBois and Akbar Muhammad, the son of Elijah Muhammad and an Islamic studies student at Al-Azhar University, with whom he had corresponded since 1961.[57] During this period in Egypt, Shabazz studied the foundations of Islamic religious traditions—the Qur'an, the Five Pillars, and so on. He was also exposed to the political interpretations of these traditions that supported the Nasserite revolution on behalf of the oppressed. That Shabazz was both invited and willing to give public speeches about religion and politics indicates the extent to which he and the SCIA had found common ground.

When Shabazz addressed the crowd at the Young Men's Muslim Association (YMMA) in Cairo on July 27, 1964, he tried to connect his own struggle to that of his audience. Founded in September 1927, the YMMA (whose Arabic name could also be translated as the Society of Muslim Youth) had from its very origins combined Islamic religion with Egyptian nationalism.[58] Reflecting the revolutionary fervor of Nasser's popular revolution in the early 1960s, the organization was an ideal setting for Shabazz to rally popular support for linking the African American struggle to the Third World liberation politics of Egyptians. It was during this speech that he offered the fullest expression of his emerging Islamic ethics of liberation.

In the version of the speech that he handwrote in cursive in his diary, Shabazz began with a religious testimonial emphasizing gratitude to God: "I am proud and thankful to Allah for blessing me to be a Muslim. Ever since I first heard about Islam and accepted it as my religion, Allah has blessed me in many ways, and with friends in all walks of life."[59] The outline of his speech, the one in which he listed the qualities of Gamal

Abdel Nasser, included the note that he was honored to "address you on [the] birthday of our great prophet of Islam: Sayyidna Muhammed (P & B)." This formulaic praise of the Prophet, including the word "Sayyidna," meaning "our master," and the phrase "P & B," or "praise and blessings be upon him," indicate Shabazz's fluency in the religious rhetoric familiar to his audience in Cairo and used by Muslims across the globe. He then expressed his gratitude for the *umma*, the global community of Muslims. "Since becoming a Muslim," he said, "I have traveled much throughout the world, to many lands and places, but I have never entered a Muslim country and felt like I was a stranger." Islam, he testified, was the social glue that bound together different people across linguistic, national, and ethnic boundaries: "I have found nothing but love, friendship, hospitality and true brotherhood wherever I have gone among Muslims, because Islam is the religion of the true brotherhood, a religion in which Allah has made all who accept *Him* look upon all of our fellow-humans as brothers and sisters."[60]

In the very next statement, however, Shabazz made clear that this Islamic brotherhood had serious ethical and political implications. It was not enough to offer words of friendship; true brotherhood had to be more than a disembodied sentiment: "One of the greatest blessings a man can have is a *true* friend, a true brother. . . . As Muslims, we want for our brothers the same things that we want for ourselves. The well-being of our brother becomes our well-being. His happiness is our happiness. . . . His pain and his sorry becomes our pain and our sorrow." Shabazz was moving the audience toward his call to action, but first he reminded them that Islam was the only force capable of forging "unselfish concern for our brothers and sisters all over the world," the kind of human solidarity that he was envisioning.[61]

Shabazz asserted that "true" Islamic brotherhood must be expressed in a form of revolutionary praxis. Egyptians were fortunate, he said, to have a living example of that praxis. "In my humble opinion," he proclaimed, "President Gamal A. Nasser reflects an excellent of the type of unselfish fighting-spirit needed by true Muslims." Shabazz made clear that, contrary to some criticisms of Nasser as irreligious or secular, the Egyptian leader was what he considered to be a real Muslim. "His [Nasser's] concept of Islam doesn't keep him from being a militant leader in the struggle against oppression," he said, echoing a thought that he would continue to express until his death: namely, that religion cannot get in the way of liberation but instead must fuel it.[62] Alluding to Nasser's leadership in the OAU and his activism on behalf of oppressed people outside of the UAR, Shabazz argued that "he has dedicated all his time and energy to restore freedom and human dignity not only to the people of the United Arab Republic but also to oppressed Arabs, Africans, Muslims as well as non-Muslims everywhere on this earth." Weaving his initial theme of Islamic religion's focus on universal brotherhood together with Nasser's policy positions, Shabazz went on to declare that Nasser's "concept of Islam forces him to fight for the liberation of all oppressed people, whether they are Muslims or otherwise, because Islam teaches us that all of humanity comes from Allah, and all of humanity has the same God-given right to freedom, justice, equality—life, liberty, and the pursuit of happiness."[63]

This statement is a hermeneutical key to understanding Shabazz's emerging ethics of liberation, which exemplified key components of American liberalism. He argued that Islam not only permits political activism but "forces" all those truly concerned about the oppressed, whether Muslim or not, to take action on their behalf. In just a few sentences, Malik Shabazz created a rhetorical arc that began with Islamic universalism, traveled through the liberal values expressed in the US Declaration of Independence, and then ended at Nasser's advocacy of independence from Western domination and white supremacy. This articulation of freedom dreams, dreams with which most Americans could theoretically identify, represented an opening in which Malcolm X's dissent could be engaged as part of American politics. Malcolm X was unwilling to accommodate racism and imperialism, but he clearly spoke the American liberal vernacular of justice and equality. The refusal of American liberals to seriously engage his ideas and advocacy meant that Shabazz had little choice but to turn to other allies for assistance in realizing Black freedom.

Shabazz made clear that Arab and Muslims in Egypt who claimed to uphold Islamic values must work for the freedom of all oppressed people of color, Muslim or not. This outreach asked for a kind of foreign intervention—even if only rhetorical—in American domestic affairs and argued that it was an Islamic religious obligation. After praising Nasser as a Muslim man of action who cared for all people, Shabazz called his audience to account. "In most areas of this earth, especially Asia and Africa, the dark-skinned *majorities* were oppressed," he said. It was even worse for African Americans, he said, because they were minorities. "In the world history of oppression, the case of 22 million oppressed Afro Americans is uniquely different," Shabazz stated. "If here on this African continent you found yourselves tortured and exploited by a European minority, right here in your own land," he added for emphasis, "imagine the pain, torture and exploitation we suffer." He declared that Black Americans are "still colonized in America by the brothers of the Europeans and they outnumber us." And then for anyone who had not yet understood what he was trying to say, Shabazz made it plain. He would always "fight for the spread of Islam until all the world bows before Allah, but as an Afro-American, I can never overlook the miserable plight of my people." He embraced a dual identity as a Muslim preacher and Black liberation activist. "So I come before you here in the Muslim World not only to rejoice over the wonderful blessings of Islam but also . . . to remind you that there are 22 million of us in America, many of whom have never heard of Allah and Islam." If Muslims were going to condemn apartheid South Africa, according to Shabazz, they were also obligated to condemn the neocolonialism of America: "In Allah's eyesight, racism must be openly condemned whether it is the open kind practiced by South Africa or whether it is the deceitful, hypocritical kind practiced by America."[64] In the version of the speech released to the public in the United States on August 6, 1964, by his assistant, James Shabazz, he also said that aiding the African American struggle was "the moral responsibility of the entire Muslim World—if you hope to make the principles of the Quran a *Living Reality*."[65] This was almost exactly the same thought that he expressed a few months earlier in a letter written from Lagos, Nigeria, in which he said that the Muslim world had an obligation to aid in the struggle for liberation of oppressed people no matter what their religious affiliation.[66]

Shabazz's remarks in Cairo demonstrated how the struggle for human rights—a liberal alternative to anti-Black racism and colonialism—would be best accomplished through the kind of political program implemented by Gamal Abdel Nasser. In this formulation, Shabazz saw no necessary contradiction between his religious and political commitments.[67] It was just the opposite. Islam, exemplified by Nasser, was not only a form of personal piety but also an ethical obligation to the rest of humanity. Its radically egalitarian nature required political and if necessary military action on behalf of the oppressed. Shabazz argued, whether abroad or at home, that African Americans in the United States were among the most oppressed peoples of the earth. Their liberation from white supremacy, like the liberation of their brothers and sisters in Asia and Africa from colonialism, was an Islamic religious imperative. It may be tempting to claim that Shabazz was merely using Islamic rhetoric, Muslim solidarity, and the institutional support that Arab Muslims could provide as a means to further the goal of political liberation and his own role in bringing it about. But that seems too cynical given the way in which this basic ethical philosophy linking religion and politics had been a consistent theme in Shabazz's life since the 1950s.[68] He had chosen to be a Sunni Muslim political activist when he could have joined any number of other movements focused on Black liberation. Even after he questioned his faith in the man whom he had once called his savior, Elijah Muhammad, he willingly became a neophyte in Sunni Islam, humbly accepting instruction from other religious authorities. Through it all, Shabazz remained committed to the idea of a liberating religion, and the state-sponsored version of Islam to which he was exposed in Egypt came closest to his own thinking. Though state-sponsored Islam—and especially the Islamic Nasserism constructed by Al-Azhar University, the SCIA, and other Egyptian institutions—would later be criticized as an illegitimate or unpopular form of Islam, this is not how many Muslims, both inside and outside Egypt, saw it in the 1960s.[69]

Shabazz's enthusiasm for this revolutionary Islam is clear in his reaction to a youth conference held on August 2, 1964, in Alexandria, Egypt. Organized by the SCIA, the Abu Bakr Siddiq Camp for Muslim Youth welcomed Muslims from around the world.[70] Often overlooked or underanalyzed in accounts of Shabazz's final year, this conference, which featured hundreds of Muslim youth from what he described as seventy-four different countries, generated feelings of religious solidarity that rivaled or surpassed those that he had experienced during his hajj to Mecca.[71] "This affair," he wrote, "impressed me even more than my trip to Mecca: youth from everywhere, faces of every complexion, representing every race and every culture . . . all shouting the glory of Islam, filled with a militant revolutionary spirit and zeal."[72]

Having learned only on the train trip from Cairo to Alexandria that he would be addressing the youth conference, Shabazz was not "only shocked, but nervous and frightened." When he arrived at the meeting place in Alexandria, he was greeted by a long reception line of youths shouting "Welcome Malcolm!" He wrote: "It was so exciting, so unexpected by me, such an honor, I hardly knew what to say or how to react." Such sentiments were almost exactly those that he expressed when he was received in a similar fashion at the University of Ibadan in Nigeria, and described in the *Autobiography of Malcolm X* as the moment when he was given the moniker Omowale, the son who has come home.[73] In Alexandria, the honoring of Shabazz was not about welcoming home a lost son but about saluting a fellow fighter in the struggle against the oppression of Africans, Asians, and other people of color. According to Shabazz, the meeting began with a recitation from the Qur'an, and then young people from Uganda, Philippines, and the United Arab Republic addressed the crowd, making "speeches of welcome and support for the Afro-American struggle." As they spoke, male and female audience members "jumped to their feet shouting beautiful slogans of support and unity in our common struggle." An SCIA official then announced that he was granting Shabazz's community of African American Muslims in the United States twenty scholarships so that they could come to Egypt to further their studies. Finally, Shabazz spoke for what he described as half an hour, followed by a speech from his translator on "the importance of doing, producing . . . *action.*" The meeting concluded with the singing of a Muslim anthem that, he said, sounded to him like a fight song.[74]

It is no wonder that the event made such an impression, since in this setting Shabazz finally heard, coming from the mouths of Muslim youth from around the world, the religious and political solidarity with African Americans for which he had been pleading and petitioning leaders at the African summit of the OAU. Indeed, Shabazz noted with satisfaction that the young Muslims expressed their support "stripped of the 'diplomacy' I had heard at the Summit."[75] Unlike the tepid communiqué that the African leaders issued in support of African Americans, the expressions of these youths were full-throated and revolutionary.

In September 1964, after Shabazz collected a credential from Al-Azhar University that certified him as a Muslim missionary, he went on to obtain similar credentials from the MWL. Once in Saudi Arabia, Shabazz performed '*umra* and underwent additional religious training.[76] His education was overseen by Shaykh Muhammad Sarur as-Sabban. As-Sabban, the descendent of Black slaves, was a former finance minister of Saudi Arabia who became the MWL's first secretary-general.[77] In his diary, Shabazz considered the idea of naming a mosque in New York after the "tall, black, very alert, and commanding" Sabban, "using his life story as the inspiration," as Shabazz put it. Shabazz also obtained pledges from Saudi officials for financial support of a new mosque and fifteen scholarships to the University of Medina for members of his community.[78]

Having conducted what he considered to be fruitful trips to both Egypt and Saudi Arabia, Shabazz then left for another tour of sub-Saharan African countries. He had meetings with eleven African heads

of state, including Kenyan president Jomo Kenyatta, and gave public remarks that focused less on Islamic matters and more on Black solidarity and neocolonialism. According to his diary, Shabazz finally returned
home to New York on November 27, 1964. He went back to work, trying
to catch up on business left undone during his long absence. Shabazz
quickly followed up with his Arab Muslim sponsors, trying to secure the
funding and scholarships offered by both the SCIA and the MWL. He
immediately cabled or wrote letters to the leaders of both organizations.
What comes through in this correspondence is Shabazz's highly strategic
and pragmatic approach to networking and fundraising with numerous
interests in the Arab Middle East, but also his preference for the Nasserite position in the Arab Cold War.

He wrote on the same day—November 30, 1964—to both the MWL
and SCIA. His plea to the MWL's Sabban was particularly critical since
an MWL missionary had appeared in New York expecting Shabazz's
community to provide hospitality and financial support. Writing from
his East Elmhurst address in New York, Shabazz began this letter with a
word of gratitude for the presence of Sudanese religious scholar Ahmad
Hassoun, an MWL affiliate who was knowledgeable about Islam, the
Qur'an, and Arabic. But he also wrote that his New York community
could not pay this religious teacher because they were "very poor." Shabazz had been under the impression that the Muslim World League or
the Saudi government would pay for the teacher's expenses, and apolo-
gized for any misunderstanding. He said it was an "embarrassing pre-
dicament." The reason for his organization's poverty, he explained, was
because he had left "all our treasuries in the Black Muslim Movement."
Shabazz then proposed a detailed budget for Hassoun and asked for at
least six months' support.[79]

In the final paragraph of the letter, Shabazz's tone became more urgent, describing the situation as a "financial crisis." In fact, he continued,
Hassoun seemed to think that the community did not want him, and he
expressed a desire to return home. Asking for an immediate response,
Shabazz assured Sabban that "I consider myself a complete servant of

yours and of the Muslim World League and I await your instructions."[80] In its tone the letter sounds humble and even obsequious, and yet it is clear that Shabazz, like fundraisers and grant writers before and after him, tailored his request in terms that he believed would increase his chances of obtaining financial support. He was adopting the voice of humility as a strategic choice, as he made clear in other correspondence written the very same day.

In a letter also dated November 30, 1964, Shabazz wrote to Muhammad Taufik Oweida, the UAR minister of *awqaf* (or religious endowments). It sought to reassure the Egyptians that his relationships with the Saudis did not reflect his deepest political and religious commitments. This fascinating letter began with words of thanks to President Nasser and the SCIA and then offered a prayer. "May Allah grant President Gamal Abdul Nasser a long life and good health," wrote Shabazz, "for he has a tremendous task ahead of him in desire to revolutionize and modernize the thinking of the Arab World, the African World, and the Muslim World." Shabazz then made clear that his own mission depended in no small part on his success in cultivating ties to Saudi-funded interests. "I have gone quite far in establishing myself and the Muslim Mosque Inc., also with the Muslim World League," he explained. "I am hoping that you understand my strategy in cementing good relations with them." And then Shabazz's rhetoric turned romantic.

"My heart is in Cairo," he declared. "And I believe the more progressive relations [*sic*] forces in the Muslim world are in Cairo." But Shabazz asserted that he could better advance the cause of Cairo "by solidifying myself also with the more moderate or conservative forces that are headquartered in Mecca." Sounding almost like an intelligence officer, he added that when he was in Geneva, Switzerland, he "even took time to speak with [Muslim Brother and Islamic Center director] Said Ramadan so that I could find out what he was thinking without ever letting him know what I was really thinking."[81]

This, too, seemed to be a strategic admission of partial truth—a spin that would reassure his Egyptian government allies that he was not going to become allies with the Muslim Brothers, which Nasser had declared to be his enemy. While it remains unclear exactly what Shabazz found attractive about Ramadan and the Muslim Brothers, his relationship with them was no passing interest. As noted above, he began to receive literature from Sa'id Ramadan's Islamic Center in Geneva as early as 1962. On April 30, 1964, after giving a speech at the Sudanese Cultural Center in Beirut and dining at the home of Dr. Malik Badri, who was his host for the 1959 visit to Khartoum, Shabazz visited the Muslim Brothers' office in Lebanon.[82] They "gave me a very touching send-off," he wrote.[83] Then, he decided to stop over in Geneva to visit Ramadan. Shabazz likely hoped that the Muslim Brothers would offer financial and institutional support to his community in the United States; after all, he knew from Dartmouth student Ahmed Osman and Muslim leader Mahmoud Shawarbi that the group had allies and some members in the United States. Perhaps Shabazz also found attractive their calls for Muslim unity as a form of politics, though he may not have wanted to say so publicly.

Whatever the case, Shabazz's relationship to these Islamists was not uncritical. He issued serious, public criticism of Sa'id Ramadan's utopian notions of race relations. In one of his very last interviews, in February 1965, Shabazz penned answers to questions that Ramadan had posed to him via post in November 1964. In this long-distance interview for *Al-Muslimoon* magazine, Ramadan challenged Shabazz to abandon his rhetoric of racial liberation. Was it true, Ramadan wrote, that you "still hold Black color as a main base and dogma for your drive under the banner of liberation?" If that was the case, Ramadan asked, how "could a man of your spirit, intellect, and worldwide outlook fail to see" that Islam affirms the equality of all people, "thus striking at the root of . . . racial discrimination?" In his response, Shabazz claimed that non-Black Muslims had done very little to convert African Americans to Islam, instead focusing on whites. In other words, Shabazz pointed out the hypocrisy of Ramadan: If Islam erases racial discrimination, then why are so many foreign Muslims still racist in their missionizing strategies?

Even more, Shabazz offered a simple rejection of Ramadan's argument that he stop focusing so much on Black liberation. "As a Black American," Shabazz wrote, "I do feel that my first responsibility is to my fellow Black Americans."[84] Such forceful language evidenced Shabazz's determination to remain independent despite his need for the assistance of Ramadan's allies in the MWL.

The rejection of Ramadan's belief that Islam erased racial prejudice was also a critique of *one* modern, liberal interpretation of religion as inner-directed and private.[85] Ramadan was implying that if everyone converted to Islam, then, miraculously, individuals would no longer be racist, and the social structures of which they were a part would thus embody racial equality.[86] The argument that racial equality might be achieved through mass conversion to Islamic religion reflected a strand of the Muslim Brotherhood's approach to social change: namely, that the Islamization of individuals through religious revival was a necessary precondition of lasting political transformation. In fact, by the 1970s, the Muslim Brothers came to an agreement with the government of Nasser's successor, Anwar Sadat, to focus on philanthropic activities such as social and medical services and missionary work.[87] A minority of Islamists outside of the Brotherhood then used violence to spur top-down political change in Egypt.[88]

Though it is impossible to know how Malcolm X would have reacted to these developments, it is clear that in the 1960s he did not believe in an individualistic religion's ability to alter the political and social status quo. Well-known for his rhetorical dismissal of pie-in-the-sky, understand-it-better-by-and-by Christianity when he was a leader of the Nation of Islam, Malik Shabazz's conversion to Sunni Islam in 1964 did not temper his criticism of individualistic, otherworldly religion. In 1964 and 1965, journalists' queries to Shabazz about whether he was becoming more religious and less political clearly assumed that religion was or at least should be apolitical.[89] Shabazz responded that "the problems of the Negro go beyond religion," as he put it to *New York Post* reporter Timothy Lee on February 18, 1965.[90] Given his other public comments about the nature of religion, he seems to have meant by this answer that the problems of Black people could not be solved by a liberal vision that confined religion to the private sphere. What was required, as he said in other instances, was a religion of praxis, as he described both in Cairo and Alexandria. "I believe in religion," he said on February 3 to an audience at Tuskegee Institute in Alabama, "but a religion that includes political, economic, and social action designed to . . . make a paradise here on earth while we're waiting for the other."[91]

The Trans/national History of Muslim American Dissent

The fact that Shabazz was using a critique of religion developed in the postwar United States to respond to the social change theories of an Egyptian Islamist activist in Geneva is only one indication of the transnational nature of his story. The politics of Malik Shabazz were boldly fashioned in a global context in which he sought to build political and religious solidarities that appealed to the hearts and minds of people outside the United States. He explicitly sought the help of Gamal Abdel Nasser, who was seen by US foreign policy officials and the liberal establishment as a destabilizing force in the Middle East and a potential danger to US national security interests there. Shabazz's Pan-African, pan-Islamic relationships attracted US governmental surveillance both at home and abroad. He may not have liked it, but he knew that this was a price he would pay to gain allies in the struggle against anti-Black racism and US militarism abroad. He refused to assimilate to a liberal political order in which he and other people of African descent could not possibly find freedom and equality, as he also continued to appeal to liberal ideas and to liberal institutions.

Even so, he was seen a grave threat by US authorities. He unapologetically lobbied foreign authorities in his struggle for rights and dignity at home. In so doing, he revealed his connection to an old tradition in African American Islam. A transnational imagination has been at the heart of Islam's rise as a Black religion since the early twentieth century, when

Islam was adopted and interpreted as a purchase on Black Americans' transtemporal and transspatial connections beyond the United States to the Muslim Orient, ancient Egypt, Morocco, India, Mecca, and even the metaphysical origins of the universe. These connections to other political, cultural, religious, and social spaces, both physical and metaphysical, were sometimes imagined in conversation with written sources about Africa and the Muslim Orient and with Muslim missionaries and immigrants. At other times, the connections were forged by African American travel and pilgrimage to the Muslim Orient, a phenomenon dating to the 1800s.[92]

But most Muslim Americans who cross national boundaries or forge alliances with Muslims abroad do not seek to challenge the nation in the way that Malcolm X did. Some anti-Muslim critics wrongly assume that connections to Muslim people and institutions abroad will somehow lead to anti-American thoughts and behavior. We saw this earlier, in the discussion of how fantasies and conspiracies about the connections of liberal Muslim Americans such as Rep. André Carson to foreign Muslim movements are often promulgated in contemporary America by professional Islamophobes. Such dirty tricks are hardly new in US politics. The tarring of domestic Muslims as agents of foreign powers has always been an arrow in the quiver of those who aim to impugn the patriotism of their fellow Americans. It is a venerable strategy dating to the very first days of the republic. And it is used by people of every political stripe.

In truth, as political scientist Roxanne Euben has observed, travel need not result in any fundamental shift in a traveler's consciousness or identity; travel is just as likely to inspire "critical distance," "sharp closure," and a "hardening of prejudices" as it is to encourage personal transformation. It all depends, Euben argues, on "a complex and mercurial interaction of the personal, political, historical, and institutional."[93] In a world whose crossings have differing effects on the structures of power, anthropologist James Clifford advocates the view that "what matters politically is who deploys nationality or transnationality, authenticity or hybridity, against whom, with what relative power and ability to sustain its hegemony."[94]

In Shabazz's case, his geographic imagination, religious identity, and political loyalties were already focused on both the Dark World and Muslim-majority countries long before he ever left for his first trip to Africa and the Middle East in 1959. During the 1950s in Harlem, Shabazz's interaction with people committed to the solidarity of nonwhite or Muslim nations and groups led him to trumpet Islam as a means of political liberation for all people of color, no matter where they lived. By 1964, he began to state more forcefully the idea that all Muslims must actively oppose white supremacy and foster Black self-determination. Having been a supporter of Nasser for years, Shabazz identified the Egyptian leader as a champion of this ethical vision, in a sense replacing the prophet Elijah Muhammad. But as a pragmatic leader of a nascent Muslim organization who desired international Muslim support and acceptance, Shabazz also cultivated close ties with Nasser's rivals. Shabazz resisted those aspects of his allies' ideologies that he found unacceptable—such as Sa'id Ramadan's insistence that mass conversion to Islam would solve the global problem of anti-Black racism—while accepting the Islamic missionary training that he found religiously and politically valuable.

After Shabazz's death in 1965, several African American Muslim groups appropriated aspects of his legacy while also adopting and adapting the political and religious practices and beliefs of foreign and American-born Muslim missionaries.[95] Among these groups were the Mosque of Islamic Brotherhood, Darul Islam, and the Islamic Party of North America.[96] New Yorker Khalid Ahmad Tawfiq, for example, was a follower of Shabazz who benefitted from one of the twenty scholarships awarded to the Muslim Mosque, Inc., by the SCIA in Cairo. After returning from study at Al-Azhar University, he established the Mosque of Islamic Brotherhood (MIB) in 1967. Tawfiq followed in Shabazz's footsteps by combining a commitment to Sunni piety with a strong emphasis on Black consciousness and self-determination. Thus, at its Harlem headquarters the MIB hoisted a red, black, and green flag—the colors of

African independence—that included a star and crescent. Throughout the 1970s, believers lived communally in Harlem and gave their children an Afrocentric Islamic education.[97] Whether seeking exile from US racism, militarism, and imperialism in a New York neighborhood or abroad, some African American Muslims who followed Shabazz's path of liberation sought to transform the political space in which they were living into one that could sustain Black humanity.

But in the coming years, most Muslim Americans, whether African American or not, would not seek exile. Malcolm X's radical vision of global Black liberation was not adopted by the Muslim American majority. His diasporic and international imagination remained vital in Muslim America, but instead of using those connections to the worldwide Muslim community and to people of color to spark a revolution against US empire and anti-Black racism, many Muslim Americans sought to reform, accommodate, or support US liberalism. This reinvestment in the American project included former members of the Nation of Islam as well as many foreign-born Muslim immigrants. As the next chapter explains, the transnational imaginations of Muslim Americans eventually inspired greater resistance to US foreign policy, but did so largely within more acceptable limits of dissent. Rather than loudly and provocatively opposing US nationalism, much of this resistance was careful to acknowledge the supremacy of the nation-state. After 9/11, however, the possibility of even tepid critique contracted in a time of war when Muslim bodies were killed or tortured by the US government at an unprecedented rate.

4

The Transnational Ethics of Four Muslim American Women in Jordan

The passage of the 1965 Immigration and Naturalization Act had important consequences for US society as perhaps over a million foreign-born Muslims immigrated to the United States by the end of the twentieth century. In the 1960s, as we have seen, the most well-known Muslims in the United States were African American men such as Muhammad Ali and Malcolm X. The movement through which both men became Muslim, the Nation of Islam, not only had the most significant media presence of any Muslim group but also operated the largest number of religious congregations and schools of any national Muslim organization. Syrian, Bosnian, Turkish, Punjabi, Sudanese, Bengali, and other Muslim immigrants had been establishing religious congregations since the early twentieth century, but now the number of mosques unaffiliated with the Nation of Islam (in addition to Isma'ili jamatkhanas and other Muslim religious congregations) multiplied exponentially. By the end of the twentieth century, there would be over a thousand Muslim American mosques and hundreds of Islamic parochial schools.[1]

This chapter explains how Muslim American politics were affected as the attention of the public and the government shifted in the late twentieth century and especially after September 11, 2001, from Black Muslims toward these "brown" Muslims, those often perceived to be from a West or South Asian immigrant background. Islamophobes then (and now) argued that these Muslims could not assimilate because Islam itself is antithetical to American culture, especially to ideals of American democracy, a belief in gender equality, and the values of religious tolerance. This chapter illuminates how, on the contrary, Muslim Americans often maintained their beliefs in these norms, even when they left the country to visit or live in Muslim-majority locales. After explaining the shifting geopolitics of Muslim American identity in the late twentieth century, the chapter focuses on the responses of four Muslim American women to the fundamental questions of political belonging that they were forced to negotiate as a consequence of the changing milieu for Muslim Americans after the September 11 attacks and the beginning of the "war on terror." Rather than examining their formal political participation, the chapter analyzes their political vision and everyday politics as they figured out how to act ethically and to practice Islam at a time when they were frequently asked to pledge loyalty to their country first and their religion second. These women, like most Muslim Americans, were not famous like Malcolm X or Muhammad Ali. But in the early twenty-first century, the problems they faced increasingly defined Muslim America at the grassroots.

Long after interviewing the four women discussed in this chapter, it became apparent to me how much the disciplinary forces of the post-9/11 era had shaped the questions that I asked and thus the answers that they gave. By using the term "disciplinary forces," I am referring to the idea that human culture is influenced, at least in part, by a variety of political interests that limit or shape the dominant ideas that people express. Those dominant ideas are often called a discourse. In the case of my research on Muslim Americans in Jordan, the discourse was not only molded by powerful concerns about Islam and Muslims in the post-9/11 era, but also by the material reality that my research was being funded through a Fulbright grant, a program of the US Department of State. The fact that I received government funds did not mean that I engaged in any form of censorship. Discursive discipline does not generally work this way in academic life, one of whose discursive norms is the idea of open inquiry. Rather, the discursive mechanism embedded in the research was the idea that I needed to defend my subjects against accusations of illiberalism in the first place. The orientalist justifications for liberal military intervention in Muslim-majority nations included racist beliefs that Muslim women were in need of saving, that Islam was undemocratic by its nature, and that Islam made its believers violent.[2]

In retrospect, I realized that my research among Muslims living abroad in Jordan sought to disprove these stereotypes. What I also discovered, however, was that the women I interviewed offered humanizing resistance to the policies of the US government and American citizens' support for such policies, as they contemplated how and why their fellow Americans could possibly support a foreign policy that led to such great suffering. Thus, our conversations during 2009 and 2010 became testaments to the impact of American liberalism's violence toward Muslim people abroad and Muslim American attempts to mitigate that reality.

The More Things Change: Muslim America before and after 9/11

By the end of the twentieth century, as Zareena Grewal has shown, many of the foreign-born Muslim Americans who had established most of Muslim America's new congregations lacked formal training in the Islamic religious sciences. But the absence of academic training in Islam did not prevent them from assuming religious authority in the powerful Islamic institutions they created. Articulating a form of Islamic reform, revival, and renewal that emphasized direct encounters with Islamic scriptures, these educators, engineers, and physicians often depicted America both as a site of displacement and as a new Medina, a place where they could practice Islam freely without fear of political repression. Unlike African American Muslims in the interwar period or after World War II, immigrant Muslims did not generally view America as a dystopia. They did, however, identify its many shortcomings, failings that they often said could be cured by an Islamic revival.[3] Their identification of Islam as a moral solution to America's social problems paralleled the voices of other American religious revivalists, such as evangelical Christians and Modern Orthodox Jews, in the late twentieth century.

The changes in the institutions and demographics of Muslim America as a whole took place amid similarly seismic shifts among African American Muslims in particular. Though African American Sunni Muslim congregations had existed since the historical era between World War I and World War II, Malcolm X's decision to create the Muslim Mosque, Inc., as a Sunni Muslim group both paralleled and advanced the establishment of other African American Sunni mosques and communities in the 1960s. Then, in 1975, the Nation of Islam itself began a transition to observing Sunni Islamic norms and practices. Early that year, Elijah Muhammad died and his son, W. D. Muhammad (also spelled Mohammed), rose to lead the organization. Over the next few years, he abandoned the doctrines that conflicted with widely accepted Sunni beliefs, including the profession of faith that Nation of Islam founder W. D. Fard was God and that Elijah Muhammad was his Messenger. He instructed believers to follow the Five Pillars of Islamic practice. Imam Mohammed even changed the name of the Nation of Islam to the World Community of al-Islam in the West—and would change the name of the group a few more times over the next two decades.[4]

The new World Community of al-Islam in the West also rejected the separatist political program outlined earlier. Indeed, W. D. Mohammed introduced US flags into the movement's mosques, asked believers to hold an annual patriotism celebration, and encouraged his members to enlist in the US military, which become an all-volunteer force in 1973. By the 1980s, he had combined his patriotism with a theory of social change that relied mainly on individual initiative rather than federal and other institutional means to achieve racial equality. Like many foreign-born Muslims who arrived after 1965, Mohammed argued that the Constitution and the Qur'an were illuminated by similar beliefs in individual rights and religious liberty. He sometimes sounded like a social conservative when he blamed society's ills on moral failure rather than on anti-Black racism. In 1991, he supported the US-led war that removed Saddam Hussein's military from Kuwait. When the war concluded, this one-time member of the Nation of Islam—who like his father went to prison for refusing induction into the US armed forces—was the guest of honor at a Pentagon ceremony where he was given official thanks by the US Department of Defense.[5] He was accompanied by Muhammad Ali.

Even though some African American Muslims continued to follow Malcolm X's path of revolution, Muhammad Ali was representative of the Muslim American majority, which sought to transform the country from within the parameters of liberalism. His rapprochement with the US nation-state began even before the transition of the Nation of Islam from Elijah Muhammad's leadership to that of his son. In 1971, after Ali won his case against the US government in the Supreme Court decision *Clay v. United States*—thus avoiding jail time for his conviction on draft evasion—he resumed his boxing career. His upset victory in October 1974 over hard-hitting George Foreman in what was dubbed the "Rumble in the Jungle," in Kinshasa, Zaire, was a comeback of epic proportions and international renown. As Sohail Dalautzai argues, the fact that the fight took place in Zaire, where the United States helped to overthrow the democratically elected prime minister Patrice Lumumba and supported the dictatorial president (for life) Mobuto Sese Seko, was an important indication of change in Ali's politics. In the 1960s, Ali had been willing to give up everything to protest US imperialism in Vietnam, but in 1974 he remained uncharacteristically silent about Mobuto, who was known as "America's tyrant."[6] Another sign of Ali's changing politics came during a December tour of the White House. Though no appointment was formally scheduled, President Gerald Ford made time to greet and congratulate the champ.[7] It was a remarkable moment symbolizing what would become the domestication of Ali's once fearsome anti-American voice. The apogee of Ali's reincorporation into the body politic came as he lit the Olympic torch in the host city of Atlanta in 1996.

The revolutionary heritage of the Nation of Islam did not disappear completely. Breaking away from Imam W. D. Mohammed, Minister Louis Farrakhan created a new version of the NOI in 1978. But his nascent organization did not capture the nation's—or the world's—attention in the same way that Elijah Muhammad's Nation of Islam had. This was neither because Louis Farrakhan was an unsuccessful missionary nor because he had toned down his rhetoric of Pan-African and anti-imperial rhetoric. In fact, Farrakhan managed to build a new institutional base for Elijah Muhammad's prophetic message without inheriting the assets or mosques of the old movement, and his appeal went beyond his small organization as evidenced by his leadership of the Million Man March in 1995.[8] The Nation of Islam was concerning to authorities, but it was not a primary focus of FBI surveillance anymore. The historical ground in which this new organization had emerged was different from the 1960s, and this new Nation of Islam no longer embodied the kind of Islamic threat that was increasing worrying US policymakers.

Instead, the focus of US policymakers had shifted to political Islam abroad. The rising appeal and power of various foreign Muslim political movements in the late twentieth century became especially important to US foreign policy during the administrations of Ronald Reagan and George H. W. Bush. Political Islam then, like today, took a variety of forms, and, when possible, the United States encouraged or even allied itself with some Islamic political groups. In Afghanistan, for example, the United States and Pakistan fought the Soviet invasion of 1979 by providing weapons and training to the Mujahideen; both the Carter and Reagan administrations appealed to Muslim Americans to support these efforts.[9] But when Islamic religion was harnessed as a political resource to overthrow US client states such as the Pahlavi regime in Iran in 1979 or to oppose the presence of US troops in Saudi Arabia during the 1990–1991 Gulf War, US policymakers began to fret. Such worries became more pronounced as the Soviet Union collapsed, and American foreign policy gurus and lobbyists touted Islam as the next existential challenge to US hegemony.[10]

The terrorist attacks of 9/11 were a watershed event. But to understand the reaction of the US government and the American people

to the attacks, it is important to realize that a variety of media organizations, think tanks, and political lobbies had produced significant
scholarship and political propaganda that established Islamophobia as
a hegemonic discourse for the interpretation of Muslim political activism for two decades before then.[11] Racist, anti-Muslim images, tropes,
and assertions constituted a powerful discourse that then framed reactions to 9/11. The most basic argument was that Islamic religion was the
cause of such attacks. Reapplying old xenophobic tropes, anti-Muslim
critics argued that Muslim Americans were especially dangerous given
their presence in the United States itself. They might not be able to
assimilate, it was said, because Islam was antithetical to American culture. A large group of activists, political philosophers, and public intellectuals, otherwise remarkably diverse, were united in their critiques
of Islam.[12]

The look of the Muslim other in popular culture changed. Its African
American visage was replaced with the vaguely "brown" and sometimes
veiled face of the immigrant Muslim living—and perhaps lurking—in
the American homeland. Black Muslims were still the victims of anti-
Muslim bias, especially those who were intelligible to the public as Muslims, but they were no longer the symbolic heart of American anxieties
about Muslims. The racism that had been directed for decades toward
African American Muslim dissidents now trained its gaze on "immigrant" Muslims.

This dynamic transition illustrated how US racism has always been
about more than a group's looks and their culture. That is, racism is
more than hatred of or ignorance about certain physical phenotypes
such as curly hair or dark skin or cultural traits such as speech patterns
or food ways. Racism is, instead, structural and institutional discrimination against a class of people who are made out to be aliens in the service
of a political agenda. After 9/11, writes Sylvester Johnson, Muslims came
to represent a "fundamental hazard to the civilizational identity—that
is, the racial vitality—of the United States as a Western (i.e., racially European) polity. Whether they were described as 'hostile to the West' (in

the language of NYPD's intelligence division) or as devoted to destroying the Western nature of the United States . . . American Muslims were relegated beyond the pale of the body politic in a long-standing pattern of colonial governance."[13]

This Muslim other was subject to "surveillance, incarceration, abandonment, torture," bombing, and banning. The Muslim other, as gender studies scholar Sherene Razack argues, was symbolically and materially "cast out" of the nation and out of civilization itself. Using the detention of Muslims at Guantanamo Bay, Cuba, as a metaphor to understand the politics of othering, Razack contended that Muslims everywhere lived in virtual and real camps in which they were not entitled to equal protection under law—they were excluded from the rest of the human community.[14] In this global camp, the idea of any right to privacy was belied by the surveillance of the US drone, the counterintelligence officer, and the FBI asset. No one—not even Muslim members of the US military— was exempt from detention and torture in military brigs, extralegal "black holes," and immigrant detention facilities.

Razack reminds us that the casting out of certain people from the human family is a hallmark of modernity's race thinking. She credits Hannah Arendt's classic *The Origins of Totalitarianism* with the observation that, in the modern age, race thinking "divides up the world into the deserving and the undeserving according to descent." Social theorist and literary critic Michel Foucault went even further, arguing that the nation-state depends on racism to justify its monopoly on legitimate violence, violence that has resulted in the deaths of millions. When race thinking is bureaucratized, nation-states have at times murdered or otherwise cast out their racial others from society; examples include "Auschwitz, the Soviet Gulag, the Rwandan genocide, refugee camps, and prisons in the United States."[15]

Given the way that modern racialization can lead to genocide, government policies and anti-Muslim populism after 9/11 understandably terrified some of the most successful Muslim immigrants. Many wor-

ried that their assimilation was no insurance against anti-Muslim prejudice, discrimination, or violence. In fact, certain markers of assimilation,
such as financial success, made the wealthiest Muslims, many of whom
were of Arab and South Asian descent, feel more vulnerable. "When
Muslims were asked whether, since the 11 September 2001 tragedy, their
lives had become more difficult," writes Abdolmohammad Kazemipur,
"those who reported the highest percentage of difficulty were not the
unemployed, uneducated, or unestablished; rather, they were those
with the highest likelihood and strongest indicators of assimilation into
American society," including those with high incomes and postgraduate
degrees.[16]

Muslim American women who chose to wear head scarves became
even more unsafe in the public square. For those Americans with anti-
Muslim prejudices, the veil transformed the American homeland—it felt
like an invasion of foreign culture. Muslim American women came to
expect dirty looks and long stares. They were also spat upon, threatened,
and in some cases assaulted. Many politicians, including conservatives,
denounced such hate crimes, seeing the wearing of a hijab as a sign of
America's religious pluralism and its belief in liberty. President Bush
made the defense of hijabi women a primary concern of his September
17, 2001, remarks at the Islamic Center of Washington, DC:

> Women who cover their heads in this country must feel comfortable go-
> ing outside their homes. Moms who wear cover must be not intimidated
> in America. That's not the America I know. That's not the America I value.
> I've been told that . . . some don't want to go shopping for their fami-
> lies; some don't want to go about their ordinary daily routines because,
> by wearing cover, they're afraid they'll be intimidated. That should not
> and that will not stand in America. Those who feel like they can intimi-
> date our fellow citizens to take out their anger don't represent the best
> of America, they represent the worst of humankind, and they should be
> ashamed of that kind of behavior.[17]

Saving Muslim women not only from anti-Muslim bigotry at home but also sexist Muslim men abroad then became one of the great political tropes of the age.

As the US government began its long fight against the threat of transnational terrorism, the veiled Muslim woman, long a symbol of anti-Muslim prejudice, reemerged as a powerful obsession. "Discourses of human rights become the justification for military adventures and imperial rule," writes Anne Norton. "The advancement of women's rights becomes the justification for invasion and nation-building."[18] First Lady Laura Bush used the president's weekly radio address on November 17, 2001, to frame the invasion of Afghanistan as an opportunity to save Afghan women. "Because of our recent military gains in much of Afghanistan, women are no longer imprisoned in their homes. They can listen to music and teach their daughters without fear of punishment. The fight against terrorism is also a fight for the rights and dignity of women." Oprah Winfrey extolled the liberation of Muslim women, too, helping to reify military intervention on their behalf as common sense—the decent thing to do. The Taliban's treatment of women had few defenders, but there was a cruel irony in invading a country in order to save its women. In her oft-cited article, "Do Muslim Women Really Need Saving?," Lila Abu-Lughod pointed out that "even RAWA, the now celebrated Revolutionary Association of the Women of Afghanistan, which was so instrumental in bringing to U.S. women's attention the excesses of the Taliban, has opposed the U.S. bombing from the beginning."[19]

As central as it was, however, the veil was not the only Muslim symbol to inspire anxiety in this era's US politics. Another ominous sign of the foreign Muslim presence on American soil was the Muslim who maintained ties with Islamic groups and communities abroad. In the decade after 9/11 the specter of Muslim Americans traveling out of the country attracted the attention and concern of the security establishment.[20] Rare images of Muslim Americans in Yemeni mountain hideouts and al-Qaeda training camps—Muslims on monkey bars—appeared and were recycled in news stories, political cartoons, and other media.[21] "Ties to

Muslim communities and organizations outside the nation," writes Sunaina Maira, "cast Muslim immigrants as potential security threats to the United States . . . or at least as immigrants whose political loyalties were suspect."[22]

The transnational Muslim was not a new phenomenon, as we saw with El-Hajj Malik El-Shabazz. Like Malcolm X and others before him, Muslim American men and women had been traveling abroad for decades. In the late twentieth and early twenty-first centuries, the number of Muslim Americans who did so was unprecedented, but these Muslim travelers became the object of intense scrutiny after 9/11. Zareena Grewal's ethnographic study of Muslim American student-travelers reveals the important implications of this travel for Islamic religious leadership in the United States, especially regarding the qualifications needed to assume such a position. Her book shows how studying abroad shifted the locus of religious authority in Muslim America away from the post-1965 immigrant reformers toward those who sought formal training in the Islamic traditions of Qur'an recitation, Islamic law, and Islamic mysticism and spirituality, or Sufism. White convert Hamza Yusuf, one of the most prominent Muslim American leaders of this new generation, argued that true Islam was to be found not in sui generis, ungrounded interpretations of the Qur'an and hadith, but in the vast archive of traditional Islamic religious scholarship found in the Shari'a and in Sufism. African American Muslim religious leaders and scholars such as Zaid Shakir, Sherman Jackson, and Amina Wadud similarly probed the archive of Islamic tradition in historically Muslim nations and institutions, and their example encouraged others to seek religious knowledge at various educational centers in the Muslim world. This embrace of tradition challenged the very structure of authority among Muslim Americans, whose congregations were often organized around the professional immigrant leaders. But it did not lead to any single understanding of Islamic religion nor to any one set of social or political views. It also did not generate one view of the United States as a homeland. Grewal writes that "debates over the nature of the transmission of traditions across time . . .

and across cultural difference . . . generate different moral geographies: some student-travelers embrace the U.S. as home . . . while others are far more ambivalent about the U.S. as a destination."[23]

Student-travelers, however, were only one category of Muslim Americans who went abroad after 9/11. In Jordan, for example, Muslim Americans sometimes sought language instruction and career-related training, often under the auspices of programs such as the US Department of State's Critical Languages Program and the Fulbright program, funded by the US government. They also moved to Jordan to start businesses or, in the case of some American-born women, to marry or migrate with their Jordanian-born husbands. Many more Muslim Americans visited their Palestinian or Jordanian relatives. Though no statistics exist to document the number of Muslim Americans who spent time in Jordan during the twenty-first century, one might speculate that it has been hundreds of thousands. For example, according to the Jordan Tourism Board, in the first three-quarters of 2010 alone, 125,424 Americans visited Jordan; tens of thousands were likely Muslim Americans.

In the 2009–2010 school year, I returned to Jordan, where I had studied Arabic as a graduate student, led a faculty exchange in American studies, and directed a study abroad program for undergraduates, to teach American studies at the University of Jordan and to conduct research about Muslim Americans who chose to visit, work, or move to the country. I sought to interview dozens of Muslim Americans about their identities, partly because I wished to prove what I thought I already knew: namely, that traveling to a Muslim-majority country does not generally turn Muslims into members of al-Qaeda. My most immediate goal was to ask interviewees to reflect on how their identities as both Muslims and Americans had or had not changed as a result of their residency in Jordan. Though I interviewed both men and women, the four people with whom I conducted my most in-depth interviews were female. This outcome was partly happenstance, but it also gave me the opportunity to discuss one of American liberalism's primary obsessions—the idea that Islam is inherently oppressive toward women and that their liberty depends on its reform or even abandonment.

The lives of these four women, all of whom are given pseudonyms here, contradict many of the tropes and themes that have informed policymaking toward, coverage of, and thinking about the potential of radicalization of Muslim Americans who go abroad. For instance, all these women's narratives confirmed the finding of sociologist Louise Cainkar that Muslim Americans who travel to or live in Muslim-majority countries do not necessarily become more religiously observant. Cainkar's study of fifty-three Muslim American youths who traveled to Palestine or Jordan to spend time in their parents' homelands showed that 42 percent reported no change in their religious observance.[24] One of the women's stories reveals that it is possible to study the Shari'a in a predominantly Muslim country without encountering anti-American, religiously exclusivist, or misogynistic teachings. The most important religious goal for all four Muslim American women whom I interviewed was to become a better, more ethical human being, whether in a Muslim country or not. Their experiences also illustrate Grewal's point that Muslim Americans do not travel to Muslim-majority countries for one specific political reason. In some cases, they are completely turned off of politics, and, in other cases, they remain completely loyal to the United States while also insisting that US foreign policy toward some Muslim populations is unjust.

In offering an analysis of these women's own thinking about how their time in Jordan influenced their Muslim and American identities and practices, I explain how the politics of Muslim Americans at home is ultimately connected to US politics and policymaking based on the liberal belief that military intervention in Muslim-majority countries is necessary to US national security and also a moral good. These interviewees were critics of such views and fervently hoped that US foreign policy concerning Muslim-majority nations would change. They also issued strong political, social, and religious critiques of Muslim cultures,

Jordan, and the Arab world. Rather than "choosing sides" or identifying with one community over another, these women expressed their loyalty to multiple communities and to equal justice for all. Just below the surface of their statements was a more explicit form of political dissent. They held to an earthly ethic of political inclusion that recognizes the full humanity of the stranger, the foreigner, the other. Their voices also help us imagine a future in which Muslim American citizens can claim multiple solidarities without the accusation of sedition.

This collective political vision warrants our attention not so much because it directly affects voting and political organizing but because it is what historian Steven Hahn has called a "relational and historical" politics that constitutes a form of "socially meaningful power."[25] These women's voices show us the everyday costs of US imperial intervention on the health and well-being of these Muslim Americans and their families. They illustrate how the dominant form of American liberalism, defined in practice as a form of anti-Muslim racism and US empire, affects US citizens and people abroad alike.

Ellen

Before becoming the director of a nongovernmental organization in Jordan, Ellen spent several years working for United Nations and NGO efforts to aid Iraqi refugees in Jordan. She was born to a white American Roman Catholic mother and a Jordanian-Palestinian Muslim father in Iowa. Like the children of tens of thousands of Palestinians in the 1980s, however, she grew up in Kuwait, where her father was a professor at Kuwait University. She attended an American school there, learning both English and Arabic from the time she was little. Her mother, though Catholic, was in charge of Ellen and her siblings' religious upbringing. "She was always asking us, Have you prayed? Have you fasted?" Ellen told me in our October 12, 2009, interview at the Fulbright House in the Shemasani neighborhood of Amman. Because her mother had not yet learned to read Arabic, she used pictures of Muslim children praying to help her children learn the postures associated with *salat*, the prescribed prayers often understood to be one of the pillars of Islamic practice. "My father, I don't remember him praying when we were young so we really didn't have him as an example," Ellen said. Occasionally, Ellen would join her mother in a prayer to Saint Anthony when something was lost around the house and needed to be found. In spite of her commitment to raising her children as Muslims, Ellen's mother remained a practicing Catholic. Her husband and children celebrated both Christmas and Easter with her. "My mom," explained Ellen, "was always finding similarities between our two religions." Both her classmates and her father's family pressured Ellen's mother to convert to Islam—an example of a Muslim practice that contradicts the Islamic jurisprudential principle that wives who are Jewish, Christian, or other "people of the book" do not have to convert. Ellen's father would always intervene and try to put a stop to the outside pressure. Ellen's religious education included a formal class at her American *madrasa*, or school, in Kuwait. Contrary to the fearful images found in mainstream American media concerning Islamic religious education, Ellen remembers her religion teacher as a kind, supportive man who introduced her to the stories of the prophets (*qisas al-anbiya*) and helped her memorize portions of the Qur'an.

In the summer of 1990, when Ellen was fifteen years old, she was on a visit to the United States when Saddam Hussein invaded Kuwait. Her family lost everything. They moved to Buffalo, New York, and Ellen attended a Roman Catholic high school where some of the nuns "were really hard on me," a reversal of her more positive experiences with Catholic nuns in Kuwait. When her class watched a movie about the Crucifixion, for example, Ellen and many of her classmates cried. The teacher turned off the TV, called out Ellen, and demanded, "How could you not believe that?" Ellen experienced this religious bigotry as part of a larger Gulf War–era prejudice against both Arabs and Muslims, illuminating the potency of such stereotypes in American culture before 9/11. "No one has any clue who they were at war with," she said, recounting comments such as "You're just all Arabs and you're all Muslims and we should bomb you all." Though her father advised her to lay low, Ellen "didn't take his advice very often." When one of her teachers said in class that people in the Middle East sell their daughters for camels, Ellen stood up in the middle of class and proclaimed, "You know I'm sitting right here and no one has ever offered camels for me and my father is not planning on selling me for camels." The teacher told her to sit down. She refused. "I said, 'No, I will not sit down.'" The teacher told her to sit down again. Ellen remained standing and asked the teacher whether she had ever been to the Middle East, or Arabia, as the teacher called it. The teacher told her that she had been to Israel. Ellen told me that she had nothing more to say after that, implying that the teacher's trip to Israel probably gave her a distorted view of Arabs.

A Buffalo mosque was a refuge during Desert Storm, the 1991 war to remove Saddam Hussein's army from Kuwait. Ellen attended various mosque events, feeling welcomed by the sound of qur'anic recitation and the call to prayer. Still, Ellen's finding refuge in the mosque did not mean an immediate increase in her piety. As important as the mosque was to her life at this point, "it wasn't enough to make me want to pray [on a regular basis]," she said. Her father encouraged her to preserve the family's cultural and religious heritage—sometimes intentionally speaking Arabic in front of Ellen's English-speaking American friends—but she felt the need to negotiate her cultural boundaries and religious practices for herself. While not committed to the daily prescribed prayers, Ellen did like praying occasionally.

The "most amazing moment of my whole life," Ellen told me, was when she prayed during a Muslim holiday in a football stadium in Buffalo. "Praying outdoors is the closest, I think the closest, I have ever felt to God," she remembered. Ellen was cheered by the fact that "in this country you can pray outside." This was surprising since she "had been so pushed down and . . . made to feel bad about who I was." Ellen also remarked that the all-city gathering was significant because of the racial and ethnic diversity of Muslims present there. "We never knew there were Black Muslims. I really felt like they were a step above because they were very religious and very cool," she said, making an allusion to the idea, popular among many Muslim Americans, that Black Muslims embody what Su'ad Abdul Khabeer calls "Muslim Cool."[26]

After Ellen graduated from high school in 1992, she moved with her family to Zarqa, an industrial and relatively poor suburb of Amman. "I hated it here," she recalled. She went to a women's university in Amman and was still miserable after two years. "People didn't want us here," Ellen explained. "It was boring. There was nothing to do." Then, in her third year of college, she got married—to her first cousin, a fact that she volunteered in our interview without any prompting. Though worried about what her mother's family would think about the marriage back in the United States, she was in love. It was love at first sight. Her husband, who would later become an obstetrician-gynecologist in Amman, saw her one day when she was visiting her paternal aunt's home. "He opened the door," Ellen gushed, "and said, 'Wow,' when he saw me. I said, 'Wow.' I kind of lost it after that." The couple soon married. They now have three children.

Ellen only began to pray on a regular basis after she gave birth to her first son and only began wearing a head scarf on a regular basis after she gave birth to her daughter. She told me that she hadn't known what she was missing, the feeling of being close to God, of being "one hundred percent supported." In addition to observing the formal prayers, Ellen reads the Qur'an on a regular basis and talks informally to God in her head throughout the day, "mostly about protecting my children." Even though she now observes pietistic practices every day, she insists that being truly religious requires ethical behavior. She gets annoyed with Muslims who judge her for letting her children listen to popular music and with what she regards as "extreme" practices that seek to limit women's mobility and styles of dress. To be "more religious" for Ellen means talking about religion with her family and applying various ethical lessons in making decisions about whether to change jobs or have another child.

Finally, Ellen insisted, "I have to tell you that my faith is very private . . . something between me and God and no one else needs to know about it." In Jordan, unlike in the Buffalo football stadium, Ellen prays at home and alone. She does not pray at work and makes up missed prayers when she returns home. Her husband points out the belief of many Muslims that praying together is a blessing, and he says that the idea of "private faith" is foreign to Islam, speculating that Ellen's exposure to Christianity is the reason she prefers to pray alone. But Ellen only began to pray alone after she had been living in Jordan for many years. She does not understand why she strongly prefers to pray in private though she tells her husband that she will not pray in groups. "He's like, 'That's not the way it should be.' And I'm like, 'Well with me, that's the way it is.'"

All things being equal, it might be tempting to side with Ellen's husband and explain her preference for private prayers as a latent expression of the Protestant-based American ideal that extols one's personal relationship with God as a necessary peak experience of human faith. But with transnational Muslims such as Ellen, who was born in Iowa but grew up in Kuwait, New York, and Jordan, the attribution of a personal practice to one geographic location ignores the ways in which religious practices travel, unattached at times to powerful institutions as they are adopted and adapted by human beings. In this respect, Ellen was like many of Cainkar's American informants in Palestine and Jordan, whose "transnational lens, informed by but not bound to Islam as practiced in the United States or in their parents' homelands, was a resource they consulted when considering what they were being taught about Islam and how they would practice their religion."[27] Or perhaps the decision to pray alone was a reaction to her Jordanian environment rather than an expression of an American cultural practice.

Ellen's life story illuminates how a Muslim growing up on two continents in the midst of war-making and injustice, experiencing dislocation and prejudice from both Muslims and non-Muslims, can nevertheless endure, prosper, and contribute to intercultural understanding and everyday peacemaking. It also contradicts the fears of policymakers that when Muslim Americans move abroad, they are likely to become more religious and more anti-American. Even after experiencing the downsides of US foreign policy and its horrible effects on her own life and the lives of others, Ellen did not become a political dissident and she did not become a religious radical. Transnational travel and her long residency in Jordan did not lead to a revolutionary or public faith such as that of Malcolm X, but rather to what she described as a private faith and life of piety.

Ellen's story also reveals the human costs of US foreign policy in the last several decades. During the Gulf War in 1991, Ellen's family was dispossessed and, to make matters worse, she faced anti-Arab and anti-Muslim discrimination at school. Later, the Iraq War of 2003 and subsequent US military occupation resulted in incredible suffering among the Iraqi people, and Ellen ended up as a leader of efforts to aid Iraqi refugees in Jordan. Though her story illustrates everyday survival and generosity in the face of US imperialism, it also illustrates how Muslims have disproportionately suffered the effects of the policy commitment to liberate territories and peoples from Iraqi leader Saddam Hussein, first in Kuwait in 1991 and then in Iraq in 2003.

Kelly

Kelly was born in California but went to high school in Oregon, where she also attended Oregon State University. Her parents raised her with what she later understood to be Islamic morals while also emphasizing that membership in a religious community was a deeply personal choice. Kelly met her husband at a 7-Eleven convenience store, where she was working to make some money in her college years. She fondly remembers her husband asking her father for permission to take her out on a date. After a few months, he proposed marriage, and the couple was married in Oklahoma, where many of Kelly's family members lived. Kelly and her husband settled in Texas. While they had agreed that their children would be raised Muslim, Kelly's decision to convert to Islam took years. She told her husband that she would learn everything about it and that if "God wants me to be a Muslim, I'll be a Muslim."

Kelly decided first to fast during the month of Ramadan and pray with her husband. They enrolled their children in a local Islamic school. Even though she was not a Muslim, she felt incredibly welcome at the school. She was especially impressed by the values that her daughter was being taught: "Everything that Islam teaches is the way that I was raised and the way I raised my kids. About being kind, giving to the poor, being open-minded and accepting of others." At the same time, Kelly liked the moral standards, especially the emphasis on sexual modesty, being taught. One day, when she and her daughter were walking through Wal-Mart, they spotted an image of the singer Madonna wearing a bra, and her daughter commented that such dress was shameful. Kelly was proud.

Her formal conversion to Islam came shortly after she prayed for a bank loan that came through. Looking back on the incident, Kelly reflected, "It's funny how you play games with yourself or with God, [but it's] because we're human, we're stupid, you know." In any case, it led to Kelly joining a *halaqa*, or study circle, at a local mosque, observing prohibitions against pork and liquor, and, a couple months after that, formally taking the *shahada*, or profession of Islamic faith.

In the late 1990s, Kelly visited Jordan for the first time and fell in love with her husband's Jordanian relatives and the deep traditions of hospitality she encountered. Kelly convinced her husband to move back to his native land in 1999. She then took jobs working for a school and the US embassy before establishing her own business.

Kelly's journey from Christianity to Islam and from Texas to Jordan, while compelling in its own right, is not a story of how, to invoke sociologist Arjun Appadurai's idea, human migration and movement leads to the instability of national identities and the legitimacy of the nation-state itself as a political idea.[28] Instead, Kelly's case shows how such movement and migration can lead to a critique of a government's policies without questioning the marriage of nation and state. Doubting the veracity of claims both from governmental and nongovernmental actors, Kelly instead seeks escape from formal politics.

After discussing her journey to Islam in our first interview on October 27, 2009, I asked Kelly about her political views during a follow-up visit on November 2. Kelly describes herself as a proud and patriotic American who thinks that most Americans are honest in their personal and professional lives. But she was also concerned about the encroachment of secularism in American public life and the US government's policies toward the Middle East. Kelly blames US policy toward the Palestinians on media that are biased against Palestinians. She also saw past American policy toward the late Saddam Hussein as an expression of oil interests. She judged US foreign policy to be hypocritical since the United States turns a blind eye toward Israel's nuclear weapons but is strongly opposed to Iran's apparent attempt to develop them. "It's not fair," she told me. "Let's be just and fair everywhere, with everybody." If the American people were better informed about their government's policies, Kelly said, they would insist on a change.

In theorizing about why the United States maintains its policies toward the region, Kelly identified personal moral failure on the part of US citizens as much as the media. For her, it is only through a deep lack of morality that a US citizen could fail to identify with the Palestinian cause and force the government to change its policies. I asked Kelly about the source of this moral failure. "I think that's Satan," she said. Kelly went on to explain that Satan is a gnawing, internal voice of temptation. When one gossips, backbites, watches immoral television programs, and commits other small immoral acts, one eventually becomes numb to the difference between right and wrong, including the actions of one's own government. Focusing only on one's own petty and selfish desires blinds one to the truth, which leads to bad citizenship.

Like many other Americans, Kelly sees governmental failure stemming from the failure of individuals. It might be tempting to analyze such critiques as a typically liberal religious perspective. American studies scholars and sociologists of religion have long identified the American jeremiad, the idea that the stain of individual sin can ruin a whole nation, as a key mode of social critique and social activism in the United States.[29] Such liberalism is also reflected in dominant modes in modern Islamic thought that stress the role of individual moral responsibility and human will as important to social progress.[30] A dominant modern interpretation of jihad, sometimes labeled as apologetic by its critics, is a case in point: whether one is in Jordan or Texas, one hears from Muslim preachers of many religious stripes the idea that true social change starts not by making war against non-Muslims but by conquering one's own demons.

This focus on the individual as the locus of social change may sometimes preclude a more structural analysis that faults institutions, including the state, as a cause of social problems or oppression. Kelly's interpretation of US foreign policy as a failure of human morality and good citizenship does not seem to challenge the legitimacy of the nation-state. She does not advocate the elimination of the American nation-state but is in favor of its reform. Kelly admires the honesty of the average American citizen and what she calls a respect for order and organization in the United States. She only wishes that the decency of the average American would guide its policies toward the Middle East.

When we discussed the events of 9/11 and the subsequent wars in Afghanistan and Iraq, Kelly became visibly upset, and I decided to pause the interview so she could catch her breath. Like many Muslims throughout the world, Kelly has trouble accepting the idea that Muslims could have actually committed the terrorist attacks of 9/11; as Gary Sick has suggested, such reactions might be seen as a "healthy form of denial" that indicates the "discomfort of virtually all Muslims with the events of 9/11."[31] Charles Kurzman offers evidence to support Sick's hypothesis, noting that in a 2006 Pew poll Muslims who questioned whether Arabs were responsible for 9/11 were more likely "to condemn suicide attacks on civilians in defense of Islam than respondents who didn't express doubts."[32] Kelly is a perfect example of this trend. While doubting that

Muslims committed these terrorist attacks, she also argues that under no circumstances could these attacks be understood as justified in Islam. Kelly's doubts about the veracity of the US government's claims regarding 9/11 are also shaped by subsequent federal prosecution of Muslim American charities and the invasion of Iraq in 2003. Because the government went to extraordinary efforts to prosecute Muslim American charities that aided the Palestinian party Hamas and seemed to trump up charges that Saddam Hussein possessed "weapons of mass destruction," Kelly wonders about the extent to which prejudice against Muslims and Arabs affects the government's policies and pronouncements regarding Muslims more generally.

But rather than becoming an activist against US foreign policy, Kelly expresses feelings of fear and uncertainty. She does not know whom to believe and told me that she tries to stay out of politics. Kelly's exposure to multiple messages emanating from multiple political interests and centers of interpretation has resulted in a disconnection from geopolitics in general. Her movement from Christianity to Islam might have led her to question her government's policies, but it did not seem to "discomfort" the category of nation-state.[33] Kelly neither questions the right of the nation-state to exist nor does she have less pride in her American ideals. Even if one insists that, beneath the surface, her distrust of the US government is a silent act of resistance against its legitimacy, Kelly's own theorizing about the impact of these events is that it has turned her off of formal politics. Kelly's moralistic reading of the failure of US politics is another example of how many Muslim Americans in the post-9/11 may have had serious critiques of US government policy, but did not translate those critiques into the kind of anti-colonial politics indicative of the Nation of Islam in an earlier era. One might even read Kelly's identification of sin as the root of bad US foreign policy in the Middle East as a typically liberal response to structural injustice: it is the failure of individuals rather than that of the nation as a whole. Perhaps this ideological reading demonstrates how assimilated many Muslim Americans are to American liberalism's professed belief in liberty for all. The idea that the very liberty of the nation-state depends on "colonial governance" through the domination of aliens, people who are excluded from the nation-state, is not really considered in this formulation.

Bayan

The case of Bayan suggests a different model of political engagement. When I interviewed her at the Fulbright House in Amman on October 5, 2009, Bayan was a grantee of the Fulbright US student program, which is designed for graduating college seniors, graduate students, artists, and young professionals. Her research was focused on how the meaning of Arabic women's literature is affected by its translation into English. A resident of a suburb outside Minneapolis, Bayan attended first grade in Saudi Arabia, where her mother was employed as an English instructor. Like Ellen's mother, Bayan's mother was not Muslim, but she married a Palestinian Muslim and wanted to raise her children to speak Arabic and practice Islam. Bayan also spent part of her childhood in the United Arab Emirates, where she completed the tenth grade. Skipping both eleventh and twelfth grades, she then enrolled in a special program at the University of Minnesota that allowed her to graduate with a bachelor's degree by the time she was eighteen years old. She came to Jordan as a Fulbrighter at the age of twenty.

Bayan is grateful that she was raised in a predominantly Arab Muslim environment where she learned to pray five times a day, read the Qur'an, speak Arabic, and praise God and the Prophet. Whether in Jordan or the United States, she prays regularly and recites the Qur'an, both silently and out loud. She hopes one day to memorize its 114 chapters. At the University of Minnesota and in other places, Bayan has served as imam, or prayer leader, for groups of women and has also recited the Qur'an in various study circles, though she is quick to point out that many women perform these duties. They do not distinguish her as a religious leader.

Like both Ellen and Kelly, Bayan sees Islam as more than a set of ritual practices, even though such practices are central to her life. Islam is also a repository of ethical principles, which Bayan sometimes sees practiced more religiously in the United States than in the Middle East. Like many other Muslim Americans, Bayan understands many Islamic and American values to be complementary, not contradictory. First, she notes that she learned the Islamic value of critical thinking, the desire to question "everything" and to look at different sources of information before coming to a conclusion, at an American university. Second, she views the United States' embrace of racial and ethnic diversity as an expression of the qur'anic teaching that God has made human beings into tribes and nations "so that you may get to know each other" (Bayan's translation of Surah 46:13). Finally, she said that American self-reliance was an important Islamic value, though she also argued that it was essential to remember those in need around you.

Bayan identifies as both culturally Arab and culturally American, but, first and foremost, she sees herself as Muslim. Having recently arrived in Jordan, she was sometimes frustrated by the fact that many Jordanians could not seem to understand how she could be American, Palestinian, and Muslim at the same time. The Jordanians' confusion stemmed in part from Bayan's linguistic abilities. When I first met her, I noted her Minnesotan accent, a fact that surprised her but which made her feel proud. Though she speaks perfectly accented upper-midwestern English, she also communicates in what is perceived as an authentically Palestinian *madani*, or urban, colloquial Palestinian Arabic. Many Jordanians, over half of whom trace their roots to pre-1948 Palestine, are surprised to find that "you speak the same way we do. You think the same way we do. But at the same time you're so connected to this American identity of yours." The fact that Bayan speaks both languages in ways that are understood to be indigenous seems to represent a form of pluralism unusual to her Jordanian friends. According to her, identity in Jordan is still largely determined by your (extended) family, your town, and your region. "I'm actually representing a face of American society that a lot of Jordanians don't get to see or don't even think about," Bayan told me. "I am a living example that American society is so very diverse."

This plural identity is sometimes a burden. Bayan explained that "people [in Jordan] do not understand how I do relate so much to my American identity. And the same goes for the United States. People don't understand how I relate to my Arab identity. It's very difficult not being from here, not being from there, not being from anywhere." She says that her feeling of not fitting in parallels the Palestinian diasporic experience more generally. "If you're a Palestinian refugee who has never been to Palestine, it's really difficult." Though Bayan is more mobile and has many privileges that some other Palestinians lack, she shares this feeling of being out of place. "I don't know where I'm going to go. . . . Am I ever going to feel at home? I have no idea. Maybe I never will. I don't feel very at home in Minnesota." Bayan's comments echo the voices of student-travelers in Zareena Grewal's study who share this fervent wish for a home.[34]

When I asked Bayan whether being in Jordan made her question her views of the United States and particularly its policies toward Israel and the Palestinians, Bayan told me that she was already aware of how such policies affect people since her grandfather, her uncle, and her cousins deal with the problem of statelessness on a daily basis. She told me that this personal experience shows that foreign policy "affects you on a very personal level in every way. When your uncle and grandfather are having problems, you're having problems too, because you are the one trying to think of ways to help them." As a college student, Bayan became active in the Palestinian movement. She was asked to speak at some rallies but declined, noting that "it requires you to scream and yell and I'm just not that kind of person. . . . I prefer to write an article or walk in protest."

How should we understand Bayan's identification with the Palestinian cause in the midst of her other forms of identity and allegiance? It might be interpreted as a form of diasporic consciousness, a feeling of attachment to a homeland or to a nation of people connected by lateral, de-centered relationships. But such categorizations, when used exclusively, ignore the ways in which Bayan herself theorizes her identity. Since

Bayan kept bringing up her Islamic faith in relation to other aspects of her life, I asked whether her faith was a source of comfort in coping with the feeling of being out of place. "It totally is," she said. "Because Islam is who I am, it doesn't matter which country I'm in or which society I'm a part of." When Bayan moved to the United States to go to college, she explained, "I needed to find my niche, I needed to find people I could relate to, but most of all I needed to find something that I could always identify with, that I could return to. . . . Islam has always been that to me."

Bayan embodies this identity to which she returns—this Islamic home—through her religious practices such as prayer, study circles, and Qur'an recitation and also in her dress. Whether she is in Minnesota or in Jordan, Bayan's one main criterion for her dress is whether it meets what she considers to be the Islamic requirement for modesty, which includes covering the hair (but not the face). In public Bayan wears either an *'abaya* or a *jilbab*, both of which are overgarments that extend from the neck to the ankles. She does not alter her dress depending on where she lives, but she does change it up depending on whether "there's a new style that I particularly like. . . . I wear whatever I want to wear here [in Jordan] and there [in America]."

Her identification with Islam as a home does not conflict with Bayan's pride in her simultaneously Arab and American identities. It does not, at least explicitly, question the legitimacy of the nation-state. Bayan's commitment to the *umma*, or global community of Muslims, does not negate her loyalty to the United States. Bayan insists instead that she is part of all these communities. Like many of Grewal's subjects, she opposes "the political status quo," holds to a "global view of justice," feels somewhat "alienated from the American mainstream," and possesses "attachments to Muslims abroad."[35] But Bayan feels most at home when she seeks acceptance from God rather than from than humankind, from her cosmic rather than her terrestrial abode. She works in peaceful, constructive, and often quiet ways to challenge what she considers to be unjust US policies. Through her very existence, she embodies the possibility of rapprochement between Arab and American cultures and peoples. Bayan is willing to name and publicly criticize the policies that contradict America's professed belief in liberty. She has more than one political or cultural identity, but she sees that multiplicity as a strength for an authentic democracy that encourages the enfranchisement of all. Earthly homes for her are temporary, and no one group has ownership of a nation-state. For her, one's ultimate home is with God.

Khadija

Like Bayan, Khadija is an Arab American woman who embraces her American cultural and political identities while also possessing a profound sympathy for Arab political self-determination. Unlike Bayan, however, she expressed a greater sense of ambivalence toward her religious identity because of the way that Muslims deal with issues of gender. Khadija was born in the Los Angeles area and had only recently graduated from a small liberal arts college in California when we sat down, first at the Fulbright House on October 1, 2009, and then at the University of Jordan on November 10, to reflect on her experiences. President of her student body, Khadija, like Bayan, had won a Fulbright scholarship. She worked with women and girls in Palestinian refugee camps around Amman, creating support networks focused on women's mental health, teaching English, and documenting women's oral histories and their folklore. Khadija's mother, a Muslim American, was born in Saudi Arabia to a Palestinian family; Khadija's father is from Libya.

Khadija was raised in the United States and did not travel outside the country until 2008. Her command of the Arabic language, while fluent, is an example of the cultural mélange that many transnational theorists have described when people cross various borders and combine their various cultural traditions. When Khadija speaks in colloquial Arabic, she combines words and syntax from Palestinian and Libyan dialects with idioms she has learned watching Syrian soap operas and other Arab media. Though this linguistic bricolage confuses her interlocutors in the Arab world, it is also an expression of Khadija's identification not only with her Palestinian and Libyan heritages but with a transnational Arab world in which persons, goods, and ideas come together to form a common, if always contested culture. This transnational Arab culture finds parallels with an old-fashioned vision of Arab nationalism to which Khadija claims stake. "My dad raised us with an awareness that these lines [national borders] are totally arbitrary and that really the Arab world is far more united through language, culture, food, political beliefs, and ideology much more so than people would like us to think," she explained.

When I asked Khadija whether her Muslim identity or Islamic practice was changing in Jordan, she indicated that she no longer attended the mosque every week. Like several of Cainkar's young informants, Khadija said that mosques in the United States were more like community centers, and she would often go not to pray but to attend a fundraiser for an Islamic charity or the Muslim American Society, a socially conservative national Muslim organization.[36] In Amman, where mosques are generally used only for prayer, Khadija faced disappointment when she tried to visit a prominent mosque and the security was so tight that she felt intimidated. She also noted that not many women in Jordan went to mosques. This was upsetting since, unlike Ellen, Khadija loves performing congregational prayer. "It's not the same to pray by yourself and to pray beside people, with someone touching your shoulder. It's like a different experience," she told me. She thought that women in Jordan were discouraged from praying together and made a point that "we all have agency here. We have a choice to make. We could all insist on going . . . but it feels like a hard fight."

Khadija's critique of the absence of women in mosques extends to her views of Islam more generally. "There are times when I feel like I have doubts about Islam . . . and my frustration oftentimes stems from women's issues." Like Muslim American and other Muslim women who separate Islam the religion, which might be feminist or womanist in theory, from Islam the culture, which is patriarchal in practice, Khadija said that the problem was with how "Islam is practiced or misapplied as opposed to the Islamic teachings themselves, which I have less issues with." She is not alone in this view; Cainkar found that "a number of youth spoke disapprovingly of the mixing of culture and religion."[37] The dissonance between how Islam should be practiced and how it is practiced sometimes leads Khadija away from Islam, and this "moving away from Islam often leaves me depressed and lonely and a little hopeless about the world." Khadija also attributed her own sense of religious liminality as a pushing and pulling between American societal expectations of individualism and Arab societal expectations of communalism, both of which she finds oppressive.

Wearing a hijab, tennis shoes, and baggy pants or sometimes an 'abaya, Khadija comes close to questioning why the burden of modesty sometimes seems to fall more on female than male bodies. "I should be able to walk in the street comfortably at all hours, feeling safe," she explained. "But at the same time I feel like I can't live those ideals [where gender does not matter]. I can't say, 'I feel like going out now and who cares if I go out alone or whatever,' because there are social constraints." In the end, she feels most comfortable wearing her hijab, carrying herself "in a certain way" to increase her "mobility." It was a habit of her upbringing, she said. Her parents let Khadija and her sister "do things that most Muslim parents didn't let their daughters do. A lot of our family friends were shocked that our parents let us live on campus . . . and our parents were like, 'We know them and we trust them.'"

But while Khadija continues to both critique and embrace various Islamic norms and practices with which she was raised, she sees her personal religiosity decreasing, not so much because of her presence in Jordan but because of the different life she discovered in college. Making a distinction between religion and spirituality—like many college students and other Americans—Khadija said that she still feels "very much spiritually aware and inquisitive and frustrated. [My] spirituality had not weakened at college." One of the reasons that she is teaching writing in the refugee camps is because she has found writing so fulfilling. "Writing has been liberating, and it has been, really honestly, it has been more cathartic than prayer," she confessed.

Khadija's presence in Jordan seemed to reflect the changing sense of Muslim identity that she began to develop in college. By November, she had enrolled in a course about *i'jaz al-qur'an*, or the inimitability of the Qur'an, at the University of Jordan's College of Shari'a. "I'm staying in this class less because of the content," she told me, "and [more] because of the professor." Analyzing the "fine threads" of the Qur'an's vocabulary was "OK," she said, but her attachment to the Qur'an was less cerebral and more experiential: for her, the inimitability of the Qur'an was mainly realized in "reading the Qur'an [itself]. That's when I'm struck by the power and magnificence of it." The real reason that she liked the class, as she said, was the professor: "I see him as a positive role model of a religious, practicing Muslim who is active in the workplace and who is passionate about human rights and who is multifaceted."

Khadija contrasted this professor of Shari'a with some of the female missionaries who had been recruiting her to an Islamic studies group in Amman. Hanging out with various members of the group whom she met through a mutual friend, "I could tell they had a sort of a cheerful aggressiveness about their recruitment," Khadija recalled. But when she attended one of the lectures sponsored by the group, she was "disappointed. I felt like my *iman* [faith] decreased after going to that, which was a little ironic." The speaker tackled the subject of religion and science, arguing that cloning was a scientific impossibility and that Darwin's theory of evolution was incorrect. "Islam turned out looking bad and a little ignorant" in this preacher's hands, Khadija thought. At this point in the interview, she further contrasted what she believed was the missionaries' parochial approach to Islam with that of her professor, whom she said was "cosmopolitan." She liked the fact that "he doesn't see the West through a prism of otherness." She explained that whereas she felt like the missionaries were unwelcoming of her and her points of view, the College of Shari'a at the University of Jordan had given her a warm reception. She appreciated their "taking you by the hand, the 'we'll do that for you and we'll do this for you."' For Khadija, that kindness evidenced the heart of Islamic practice, which rests in ethical behavior. This is "how I want religion to be. I actually look at the end and what matters most is how I treat people. So if something makes me treat people well, I really respect that."

Khadija paints a completely different picture of Shari'a education than the one constantly promulgated in both liberal and conservative US media. This young American woman who speaks funny colloquial Arabic was embraced by the professors and students of a Shari'a college. The open-minded nature of her male professor, her model of what a religious, practicing Muslim should be, makes the school a social space in which Khadjia can explore her Muslim identity without feeling condemned for her free-thinking ways. Even as she continues to question what for her is the problematic nature of women in Islam, she is also able to experience a positive connection with a mainstream institution of Islamic higher learning, a relationship that seems at least to reassure her that it is possible to practice the kind of ethically focused Islam to which she is devoted.

Khadija's experience studying Shari'a in Jordan is a necessary reminder that a Muslim committed to the careful study of Islamic law can also be committed to participating in US democracy. Studying Islamic law does not automatically lead one away from the ideals of American liberalism. Quite the opposite is true: Khadija's exposure to a free-minded Islamic law professor encouraged her to pursue the issue of women's empowerment—one of the most cited liberal criticisms of Islam—within an Islamic context. Contrary to stereotypes about Islamic law, her study of it also did not lead to any cognitive dissonance between being fully Muslim and fully American. In practice—as opposed to the fantasies of Islamophobes—there is no necessary conflict between the two.

American Islam and American Liberalism

Khadija's theorizing about her Muslim identity and the ways in which her residency in Jordan was or was not changing her views is, like all of stories above, evidence that travel does not necessarily lead to any questioning of political loyalties or foundational political beliefs. None of the four women expressed gnawing doubts about the nation-state's legitimacy, and I did not press them on the issue since I did not want to produce research that sustained stereotypes about potential conflicts between political and religious loyalties. None of them expressed a full-throated criticism of American liberalism, including individual rights of free speech, religion, property, and so on. Indeed, they generally associated these liberal values with Islamic religion and American culture. Clearly, *these* liberal values did not challenge their Muslim identities or what they believed to be the proper of interpretation of Islam.

Their problem with liberalism was different. It was that during the war on terror, like during the Cold War, the dominant discourse of American liberalism identified their Muslim identities and their Islamic religious commitment as threats that must be targeted for liberation or containment. Rather than seeing this Islamophobia as a structural problem—as the very warp and weft of liberalism—Kelly explained US foreign policy as the moral failure of individuals and the triumph of Satan. It was individual ethical failure, not a systemic or foundational problem with the American nation-state. And even though Bayan had harsh criticisms of US foreign policy, she did not call for its destruction or for the creation of a new polity, but rather she dreamed of a democracy that did not punish those whom she loved in Palestine.

Paying attention to the making of the Muslim American political imagination outside formal political participation also suggests how some Muslim Americans are theorizing alternatives to an American liberalism that supports and is supported by the war on terror. All of these women embrace ideals of liberty and justice to a greater or lesser degree. But they believe that all humans, and not simply Americans, deserve political rights. Loyalty to the United States does not mean that they must relinquish their solidarity with other peoples, especially Palestinians. Indeed, their ethical commitments demand that they speak out on behalf of those whom their country wrongs. Such criticism comes close to dissent, though outright opposition to US foreign policy after 9/11 can be costly, attracting government surveillance and popular accusations of sedition. The questions that I asked produced answers generally geared toward reducing American anxieties about the loyalty of Muslim Americans, but they did not allow for a fuller range of dissent. Instead, these women articulated a politics of everyday resistance to US empire. They held onto their multiple, sometimes conflicting identities as Americans, Muslims, Palestinians, Jordanians, and/or Arabs. They seemed to dream of a world in which such identities will no longer be at odds.

Whether or not this was a widely held view in Muslim America during the first decade of the twenty-first century, such utopianism was only one possible response to the war on terror. Even if they believed in a more peaceful world, some Muslim Americans also embraced a more traditionally liberal politics that supported US military intervention abroad, including in Muslim-majority countries. The next chapter describes two Muslim American youth who attempted to combat anti-Muslim prejudice by joining the US military. They took the lives of others—and their lives were taken while fighting against other Muslims. They reacted differently to liberalism's promise of political incorporation than did Kelly, Bayan, Khadija, and Ellen. Rather than pushing (even slightly) against war in the name of freedom, these men made the ultimate sacrifice in order to achieve full citizenship. Even then, it was not enough.

5

Blood Sacrifice and the Myth of the Fallen Muslim Soldier in US Presidential Elections after 9/11

In the US presidential elections of 2008 and 2016, the blood sacrifice of two fallen soldiers named Khan became part of a new national myth, the myth of the fallen Muslim soldier. In the election of 2008, retired general and former secretary of state Colin Powell was the chief poet of such mythmaking; in 2016, it was Democratic candidate Hillary Clinton. In using the label "myth" to interpret the meaning and function of stories about fallen Muslim American soldiers, I do not mean to argue that such narratives are in any way empirically false. Corporal Kareem Khan and Captain Humayun Khan, both of whom were killed in battle during the Iraq War, were real people. But narratives of their sacrifice were rendered mythic as they became part of public discourse about the meaning of communal belonging and national identity in the post-9/11 era; the blood of these US Muslim military members was transformed into an oblation that could redeem the nation.[1] Myths, as Bruce Lincoln argues, are a rare "class of stories that possess both credibility and authority." Like historical narratives, myths contain claims that are truthful to those who believe in them. But myths do more than simply recount a truth; myths also express social authority. They contain "*paradigmatic* truth"— that is, a truth that sets forth a "model," even a "blueprint" not only for individuals but also for society. Myths have been essential to the social life of human beings: by making myths, people "evoke the sentiments out of which society is actively constructed."[2]

Muslims and Islam have always been vital to American society's mythmaking. Anti-Muslim or Islamophobic myths have played a noteworthy role in the making of US national identities since the country's founding.[3] Rooted strongly in apocalyptic Christian visions of Muslims and

Islam as the anti-Christ, the myth of the superhuman Muslim "beast" first became a popular way of understanding real and imaginary Muslim adversaries in colonial New England. To be clear, racist claims about an entire class of human beings are repugnant, but, like other racist ideas, these beliefs have been held by many Americans. For those Americans, the myth of the Muslim monster is both credible and authoritative. They have adapted the mythic Muslim antihero to respond to foreign policy challenges concerning the Ottoman Empire in pre–Civil War times, the US invasion of Mindanao in the Philippines, US support for Israel during the Arab-Israeli War of 1973, the Iranian hostage crisis in 1979–1980, the first Gulf War, and the post-9/11 war on terror. Throughout these moments, and at other times, the myth of the Muslim monster has been invoked to justify violence against Muslims abroad and has also worked to define American national identity at home: "they" are violent, misogynistic, despotic, medieval, and untrustworthy, whereas "we" are peaceful, pro-woman, democratic, modern, and honest.[4]

But the myth of the fallen Muslim soldier after 9/11 challenged these anti-Muslim claims and sought to alter the symbolic role of Muslims in the making of US national identity. As Bruce Lincoln points out, myths can be used to sustain and support the political status quo or they can be used to contest it.[5] In the case of the fallen Muslim soldier, a different kind of story about Muslims in the United States was offered to displace the older myth of the Muslim beast. In this new liberal myth, Muslims would play the role of heroic patriot, and, in exchange, the nation would owe them and all Muslim Americans social acceptance and an opportunity to become part of the multicultural melting pot.

Such mythmaking is but one vital element of what Robert Bellah called American civil religion. Historian Jonathan Ebel defines American civil religion as the "narratives, symbols, practices, and institutions that create and sustain a sense of America's special purpose and place in the world"—in short, a religion of American exceptionalism.[6] Rooted in the colonial founding of the Massachusetts Bay Colony, where Puritans articulated the idea that they were chosen by God to occupy the land,

American civil religion's essential doctrine has been that America is a force for good, acting not only in the US national interest but for the sake of the whole world.[7] As Ebel points out, members of the military play especially important roles in the cultural practices that constitute American civil religion: "The ubiquity of soldier veneration is staggering, its gravitational pull tremendous: political events, parades, civic gathering of all types, car bumpers, novels and films."[8] Members of the military shape the meaning of their lives and their deaths to a certain extent, but other powerful institutions and individuals are sometimes able to narrate the lives of military members in ways that dominate public discourse. Edward Linenthal shows, for example, how over time certain images of soldiers dominated American memories of specific wars: the "Minuteman" volunteer of the American Revolution; the honorable, sacrificial soldier of the Civil War; and the "homely hero" of World War II.[9]

In the post-9/11 era, the Muslim American service member emerged as one of those powerful images. The fact that the Khans were both Muslim immigrants was essential to the new myth. Even though African American Muslims had been defending the country since the War of 1812, if not the American Revolution, their symbolic utility to the myth of the fallen Muslim soldier was limited in the post-9/11 era.[10] In the twenty-first century, Islam's foreignness in US culture was represented mainly by Muslims who were perceived to be brown, Middle Eastern, or South Asian. Americans constructed Muslims as a race that embodied a foreign, threatening presence in the nation.[11] It was precisely because the Khans looked like the very "foreign" Muslims against whom the United States was fighting that US politicians such as Colin Powell and Hillary Clinton could employ their memories in myths of incorporation that echoed successful immigrant narratives. Conjuring images of these soldiers' graves in order to renew the myth of a liberal, multicultural consensus, Democratic candidates and their supporters cast themselves as the most authentic practitioners of a faith in a religiously tolerant American nation.

This chapter argues, however, that liberalism once again failed Muslim Americans. Liberalism failed to make America safe for Muslim

American citizens because it was defined at its very core by its racist, imperial wars—all conducted in the name of freedom—that turned Muslims into the religio-racial other. By focusing on the incorporation of foreign Muslim blood into the nation, politicians such as Powell and Clinton offered a partial, ambiguous acceptance—one that both embraced and rejected Muslims as part of the American body politic. By emphasizing the importance of gaining Muslim American support in the war against terror, US politicians pointed to the very liminality of Muslim Americans. Muslim Americans were on the front lines, part "us" and part "them."[12] Somewhat suspect—valuable precisely because of their nearness to the enemy—Muslim American service members proved, by their blood sacrifice, that the US war on terror was just and right. Perhaps their symbolic sacrifices even sanctified US military intervention in the Muslim world and thus unintentionally legitimated the wars that were an essential element in the cycle of anti-Muslim sentiment in the United States. Whether or not this was the case, I argue, the myth of the fallen Muslim soldier had limited effectiveness in national discourse, as its authority was rejected by supporters of Donald Trump and Muslim activists alike. The chapter concludes by analyzing the limits of the myth's success, as some Muslim American critics called out Hillary Clinton's campaign as stigmatizing and ultimately dehumanizing, while many Trump supporters disagreed with the underlying premise that Muslims could or should be incorporated into the nation. In either case, Muslims were made into liberal democracy's others, people undeserving of freedom, victims once again of white supremacy.

Corporal Kareem Khan and the Election of 2008

On October 19, 2008, a little over a fortnight before the November 4 election contested by Democrat Barack Obama and Republican John McCain, General Colin Powell, former Republican secretary of state and retired chairman of the Joint Chiefs of Staff, appeared on the NBC News Sunday morning program, *Meet the Press*, to endorse the Democrat.

Powell outlined multiple reasons for his choice, many of which were driven by sober policy concerns and a sense of which person was better suited for the job. But there was also a "push factor" behind his choice. He had grown weary of anti-Muslim rhetoric in the Republican Party and the attempts to tarnish Obama as a Muslim. Powell pointed out that Obama was a Christian, but in perhaps the most dramatic moment of the interview, he asked rhetorically: "What if he is? Is there something wrong with being a Muslim in this country? The answer is, 'No, that's not America.' Is there something wrong with some seven-year-old Muslim American kid believing that he or she could be president?"

The reason for his dramatic declamation on this point was, he said, because of a powerful image. It was a photograph of Kareem Khan's mother at her son's gravestone in Arlington National Cemetery. Powell continued:

> And as the picture focused in, you could see the writing on the headstone. And it gave his awards—Purple Heart, Bronze Star—showed that he died in Iraq, gave his date of birth, date of death. He was 20 years old. And then, at the very top of the headstone, it didn't have a Christian cross; it didn't have the Star of David; it had crescent and a star of the Islamic faith. And his name was Kareem Rashad Sultan Khan, and he was an American. He was born in New Jersey. He was 14 years old at the time of 9/11, and he waited until he can go serve his country, and he gave his life.[13]

This image of a mother at her son's grave spoke to Gen. Powell's deepest values as a patriot and his most fervent hopes for his nation.

As numerous scholars of religion and nationalism have argued, the willingness of citizens to sacrifice their own blood for the nation and for parents to sacrifice the blood of their children might be considered the ultimate act of religious piety in the modern world.[14] World War I poet Wilfred Owen called it the "old lie," and mocked it, but also recognized the power of this act of national devotion: "*Dulce et decorum est / Pro Patria Mori*," he wrote.[15] How sweet and fitting it is to die for one's country. Carolyn Marvin and David Ingle have asserted that the sacrifice of one's life, the shedding of one's blood, is "the holiest ritual of the nation-state."[16] There is no better example of this sentiment than the French national anthem, "La Marseillaise," which asks all citizens to take up arms, form battalions, and "let an impure blood soak our fields." For Marvin and Ingle, "Christians may have been willing to die for their faith" in the past, but the God of the nation-state has replaced the God of Christianity as the ultimate basis for communal formation and social agency. Agnieszka Soltysik Monnet riffs on this idea, stating that "while many people have abandoned religious beliefs and practices, it is almost impossible to have no nationality. Even people who have lost their citizenship one way or another usually consider themselves as 'belonging' to some nation in at least a spiritual and cultural sense."[17]

This is not to say that other forms of communal formation and social belonging have disappeared in the modern world. Transnational ties of confessional religion, ethnicity, politics, race, and global economic interests exist alongside the nation-state, sometimes challenging its hegemony but more often than not sustaining it.[18] In the modern world, these social formations are just as apt to accommodate, or in the case of capitalism, reify the nation-state as the most powerful institution of human community-making. This is true even in the case of Islamist political formation.[19] In the end, according to Monnet, "nationality is generally the first and most important way that social life on this planet is organized."[20]

Religious studies scholar C. Travis Webb agrees that nationalism is a powerful civil religion—and he emphasizes the idea that nationalism is not *like* a religion; it is a religion. But Webb asserts that nation-states have not completely eliminated other religious commitments so much as they have subordinated and sequestered them to the private sphere. He points to the eighteenth-century French philosopher Jean-Jacques Rousseau's work, *The Social Contract*, as theorizing this relationship between nationalism and other forms of "translocal, supra-kin communities": "In arguing for a civil religion, Rousseau offers an interpretation of European history that legitimizes the rising power of the state over and against the declining power of Catholic institutions." Rousseau was not advocating the "abrogation" of confessional religion in favor of secularism; according to Webb, he was arguing for what he regarded as a more authentic form of Christianity, one that would not be sullied through its participation in the public sphere. He provocatively suggests that Rousseau's vision for modern religion is a form of henotheism—that is, the belief in the worship of a single god while also acknowledging the existence of other gods. According to Webb, Rousseau's "privatization of worship, and his reimagination of Christianity's historical development turns the plethora of vernacular Christianities (i.e. sectarian Christian practices) that flourished on the other side of the Reformation into what are effectively 'household gods.'"[21] Citizens are free to worship any god they like so long as their veneration of or devotion to that god does not challenge the ultimate public authority of the national god: the nation-state itself. The modern state thus tends to define "good" religion as a religion that makes people into better citizens.

Jonathan Ebel shows, for example, how American nationalism and Christian confessionalism have gone hand in hand for many members of the US military. Christian Americans have often understood service members as Christ-like saviors of the country, the "Word" made flesh. "A barely submerged incarnational theology, frequent invocations of theories of atonement, regular equations of the fallen soldier to Christ crucified are," he observes, "appropriations from Christian tradition that give both coherence and binding power to a religious tradition focused on the worship of the nation." Ebel goes further, arguing that American civil religion's "analogy, symbol, myth, and ritual" actually encourage "a Christian identity."[22]

That may be true for some, even most in the military, but not for its Muslim American members. General Powell's testimonial shows that it is not the specific confessional identity of service members that matters but rather the fact that the faith has become American. In Powell's civil religion, the nation is, quite literally, the ultimate source of meaning: who or what you are willing to die for evidences your communal affiliations.

Powell made the case on national television that the blood sacrifice of a Muslim American soldier for the nation was particularly meaningful in an era of anti-Muslim prejudice. His advocacy for the inclusion of Muslims in US nationalism echoed his own role in the military history of the United States.[23] As the first African American officer to become chairman of the Joints Chiefs of Staff, Powell signified the promise that America's military could embody, represent, and even heal a nation of many races and ethnicities. Analyzing his role in the first Gulf War during 1990 and 1991, Melani McAlister argues that "Powell became . . . the nation's premier citizen-soldier, the living embodiment of the institution in which the whole nation must recognize itself."[24] Liberals and conservatives alike lauded Powell's performance both during and after war. Powell's willingness to lead this war was understood in ways similar to the military service of African Americans, Japanese Americans, Native Americans, and other nonwhite military service members in the past: it was seen as proof of America's multicultural promise and its essential fairness and goodness as a democratic state. Like other nonwhite service members before him, Powell embodied a multicultural vision of the United States that was tied inextricably to military intervention.

Thus Powell's eulogy of Kareem Khan echoed his own symbolic meaning to American nationalism. In praising Khan, Powell was doing more than including Muslims in a liberal and multicultural vision of the US nation-state, just as his own presence meant more than having a racially integrated military force. Powell was also justifying, indeed sanctifying, wars in Muslim-majority lands as part of the myth of American exceptionalism. Khan's outsider status as a Muslim—the fact that he was fighting as a Muslim against other Muslims—signified the religious importance of America's "mission" in the twentieth and twenty-first centuries. Powell made the point that it was Muslims who now renewed the American civil religion.

Left unsaid in Powell's remarks, but essential to the making of Kareem Khan into a mythical figure, was the gendered nature of the image. One of the primary reasons Powell noticed the photograph at all was the presence of Khan's mother, Elsheba Khan. She was the one who inspired the professional photographer, Platon, to take the photo in the first place. "One day I saw this lady," he remembered. "And every day she goes to his son's grave. She sits in front of her son's grave and reads to him." Platon asked if he might take her photograph, and "she took the book that she was reading and placed it at the base of the headstone, and got behind the stone and cuddled it as if she was embracing her son."[25] In the photograph, her eyes are closed. Her left arm is stretched out across the top of the gravestone. She rests her head on her left arm as she uses her right arm to hold onto her son's gravestone.

It was a reenactment, according to Ji-Young Um, of the Pietà, Michelangelo's sculpture in Saint Peter's Basilica that depicts Mary, the mother of Jesus, embracing her dead son. "Like the Virgin Mary of the original pietà," Um argues, "she sacrificed her son without protest, calmly accepting her role in the larger narrative of collective national suffering and the redemptive figure (the son/soldier) who would die in the place of others so that they would be saved." Um points out that Elsheba Khan's ethnic and racial identity is perhaps understated in the black-and-white photograph but that Powell, the embodiment of multicultural liberalism, makes it clear that Khan and his family are part of the larger narrative of multicultural sacrifice for the nation.[26]

As a mythmaker, Colin Powell divorced narratives of American exceptionalism from their explicitly Christian theological roots. He remade the myth into a religiously plural story, as his interpretation of Arlington National Cemetery demonstrates. Powell's allusion to the presence of an Islamic star and crescent on Khan's gravestone and its implied nearness to the symbols of the Christian cross and Jewish Star of David established a solemn setting for his vision of a multicultural America. The crescent and the star proved that Muslims could be loyal to the United States, challenging the idea popular among some American voters that Muslims are inherently anti-American.

This is exactly what Kareem Khan had yearned for. Growing up in Manahawkin, New Jersey, so close to the fallen towers of 9/11, Khan had vowed to show the world that "not all Muslims were fanatics and that many, like him, were willing to lay down their lives for their country." This was no empty promise. As a high school freshman, he registered for the Air Force Junior ROTC, or Reserve Officers' Training Corps, but he ended up enlisting in the US Army once he graduated from Southern Regional High School in 2005.[27]

For twenty-year-old Kareem Khan, military service was a way to prove that he belonged in and to America; it offered what Monnet calls "the promise of unassailable national credentials."[28] Ji-Young Um adds that such service "has an intimate connection to formal citizenship as well as to symbolic citizenship." As Um observes, military service often expedited pathways to citizenship after 9/11 as the US military sought to recruit native Arabic speakers and other linguists.[29] This connection between Muslim military service and US citizenship, both formal and informal, dates to the Civil War. For foreign-born Muslims, World War I proved to be an important pathway to naturalized citizenship for hundreds, if not thousands of Muslims who might not have otherwise achieved it. In the 1920s, Arab American leaders, both Christians and Muslims, emphasized their service and their support of war bonds during World War I as proof of their contributions to the nation.[30]

As Kareem Khan knew, however, the ultimate proof of belonging to the nation is the willingness to die in battle—and to kill others "for the sake of its self-preservation."[31] During his deployment in Iraq, Khan's favorite movies were reported to be *Letters from Iwo Jima* and *Saving Private Ryan*. Both of these films arguably depict the cruelties of war as redemptive or at the very least honorable, linking the fate of the nation—one Japanese, the other American—to the (all-male) brotherhood that exists among military service personnel and their willingness to sacrifice to save a fellow soldier, sailor, or marine. Like those service members, Kareem Khan was stationed on the front lines. His job was to go house to house looking for insurgents. A member of the First Battalion, Twenty-Third Infantry Regiment, Third Brigade, Second Infantry Division, part of what is known as a Stryker brigade combat team, Khan sent emails to his family that expressed a deep commitment to the mission. On August 6, 2007, he was killed when a bomb exploded as he was attempting to clear a house in Baquba.[32]

Kareem Khan was an outsider who was symbolically incorporated into the American body politic as he was laid to rest in Arlington National Cemetery and memorialized by Colin Powell. But this was not the end of the story. The myth of the fallen Muslim American military member was no passing symbol in the post-9/11 era. Khan's memorialization as a fallen son mourned by his mother and a nation became a sign that was deployed once again in the election of 2016. Oddly, the last name of the soldier was once again Khan. But this time around, the mythmaking was even more prominent on the national stage and revealed not only the power of the myth but also its limitations to achieve national unity.

Captain Humayun Khan and the Election of 2016

On the final night of the Democratic National Convention in Philadelphia, Pennsylvania, Muslim American parents Khizr and Ghazala Khan took the stage at a dramatic moment. Attorney Khizr Khan would deliver the convention's closing argument for Hillary Clinton's campaign. The Khans were given a prime spot in the convention, appearing immediately before Chelsea Clinton, the candidate's daughter, introduced her mother as the party's official candidate for the presidency. As Khan faced thousands in the crowd and millions of viewers at home, an image of their fallen son, Army captain Humayun Saqib Muazzam Khan (1976–2004), was shown on a large screen behind them. They both wore blue, the traditional color of the Democratic Party.

Khizr Khan's speech reiterated the myth of the fallen Muslim American military member and its symbolic centrality to American nationalism in the post-9/11 era. Introducing himself and Ghazala as "patriotic American Muslims with undivided loyalty to our country," he expressed his gratitude for the opportunities that the nation had provided to his three children. He also signaled his willingness to accept that his son had to die so that others might live. Humayun, he said, put aside his own dreams "the day he sacrificed his life to save the lives of his fellow soldiers." Khan expressed his gratitude that Hillary Clinton had noticed his sacrifice: "Hillary Clinton was right," he said, "when she called my son 'the best of America.'" Clinton had made a point in earlier campaign speeches of holding up the willing sacrifice of the twenty-seven-year-old Muslim American as exemplary.[33]

Capt. Khan's death was indeed selfless. The soldiers under his command in the First Infantry's 201st Forward Support Battalion were charged with guarding the gates of Forward Operating Base Warhorse in eastern Iraq. Over a thousand Iraqis worked at the base as civilian employees. The beginning and end of their work shifts were dangerous because Iraqi rebels would exploit these opportunities to attack the base with car bombs. Capt. Khan's unit had mistakenly shot some Iraqi drivers whom they thought to be insurgents, and Khan was determined to reduce needless casualties while also protecting those under his command. He was willing to work even on his days off, including June 8, 2004. That day, he saw a suspicious taxi making its way through the serpentine barriers in front of the base entrance. He commanded his soldiers to back off and to get down. Khan signaled to the driver to stop. He approached the car. A bomb went off, killing him, two insurgents, and two Iraqi civilians. Posthumously awarded both a Bronze Star and Purple Heart, Khan was laid to rest in Arlington National Cemetery in a ceremony that included Islamic funeral prayers.[34]

As he interpreted his son's death for a national audience in 2016, Khizr Khan evoked the sacred ground in which his son's body had been laid to rest. He accused Donald Trump of profaning a holy place, asking rhetorically, "Have you ever been to Arlington Cemetery?" If he had, said Khan, he would have seen "the graves of brave patriots who died defending the United States of America. You will see all faiths, genders, and ethnicities." This discussion of Arlington is another indication of the mythmaking involved in memorializing the war dead, as it appeals to the power of the nation's most sacred cemetery. Military cemeteries evidence the power of blood sacrifice to save the nation, as Abraham Lincoln argued when he dedicated the cemetery at Gettysburg: "We have come to dedicate a portion of this field as a final resting place for those who here gave their lives that this nation might live." As Monnet points out, Lincoln "articulated one of the most enigmatic paradoxes of national identity: namely, that it is strengthened by the lives that are lost in its name." For the nation, it was a "new birth."[35] Khan's evocation of his son's final resting place both renewed the power of this myth and attempted to use it as a political weapon.

Trump violated the national faith in another way, according to Khan. If Donald Trump were successful in banning Muslims from immigrating to the country, Khan said, the nation would be deprived of those willing to sacrifice for it. Trump's prejudice rested on his own ignorance of or blatant disregard of the nation's holy text, the Constitution. Khan scolded Trump: "Let me ask you," he said, "have you ever read the US Constitution? I will gladly lend you my copy." Naming Trump as an American who had shirked the duty of blood sacrifice for the nation, he told Trump that "you have sacrificed nothing and no one." And he concluded by asking fellow Americans, immigrants, and Muslims "to honor the sacrifice of my son" by voting for Hillary Clinton.[36]

Rather than addressing any of the substantive issues raised by Khizr Khan's speech, Donald Trump insulted Ghazala Khan, who had not spoken at the convention. "If you look at his wife," Trump told George Stephanopoulos of ABC News, "she was standing there. She had nothing to say. She probably—maybe she wasn't allowed to say. You tell me. But plenty of people have written that. She was extremely quiet. And it looked like she had nothing to say."[37] In other words, according to Trump, Ghazala Khan was another oppressed Muslim woman whose husband had denied her the chance to speak.

In response, Hillary Clinton's campaign accused Trump of dishonoring a Gold Star family, and even some Republicans criticized Trump for his lack of respect. One of them was retired Major General Dana J. H. Pitard, Capt. Khan's senior officer. "My family has been Republican ever since my maternal grandparents migrated from Jim Crow South Carolina to Philadelphia in the late 1920s," he stated. But party shouldn't matter when it comes to respecting the Khan's family sacrifice. "I join all those who stand in support of the Khan family. This family is our family, and any attack on this wonderful American Gold Star family is an attack on all patriotic and loyal Americans who have sacrificed to make our country great." For Gen. Pitard, the Khans were off-limits. "Any politically or racially motivated attack on the Khans is despicable and un-American."[38]

Ghazala Khan herself also spoke out to reject Trump's insult. In a *Washington Post* op-ed, she explained why she decided not to speak at the convention:

Every day I feel the pain of his loss. It has been 12 years, but you know hearts of pain can never heal as long as we live. Just talking about it is hard for me all the time. Every day, whenever I pray, I have to pray for him, and I cry. The place that emptied will always be empty. I cannot walk into a room with pictures of Humayun. For all these years, I haven't been able to clean the closet where his things are—I had to ask my daughter-in-law to do it. Walking onto the convention stage, with a huge picture of my son behind me, I could hardly control myself. What mother could? Donald Trump has children whom he loves. Does he really need to wonder why I did not speak?[39]

Just as Platon's photograph presented Elsheba Khan as a maternal figure who mourned her son by silently embracing his tombstone, Ghazala Khan discussed her own mourning in maternal terms. Because of her motherly grief, Mrs. Khan said, she was unable to speak at the convention. Instead, she offered a silent witness, standing next to her husband, testifying to her devotion.

Strangely perhaps, Donald Trump also remained silent about the incident after his initial response. Such silence can be interpreted in a variety of ways. For one, some members of the military and veterans, including Republicans, found Trump's comments to be at the least distasteful. But it is also tempting to conclude that, for Trump, there was nothing more to say because he found the symbolic blood sacrifice of Muslim service members to be meaningless. It did not gel with his myth of America. Trump's vision of "making America great again" did not include the multicultural liberal consensus that Clinton was reaffirming. He did not seek to include Muslims in the body politic; his policy banning Muslim immigration sought to keep them out.

Though Trump remained silent about Humayun Khan during the fall, some partisans developed a more robust critique of the use of this fallen Muslim soldier as part of Clinton's campaign. One was *Drudge Report* staffer and *Breitbart News* contributor Charles Hurt, who claimed that Hillary Clinton's campaign had tricked Khizr Khan. Her "campaign was all too eager to take advantage of him and his family," he wrote. Hurt acknowledged that Khizr Khan was a "fine American and the father of a true American patriot." But Khan shared some of the blame for "allowing his dead son to be used for the most hideous of purposes and dragged through the gutter of nasty and dishonest partisan politics." This was a telling line, as Hurt attempted to wrest Humayun Khan's sacred memory from the Clinton campaign by claiming that Clinton's politicization of Khan's story had profaned his service. "For just about every American alive, Capt. Khan is an inspiring and unifying figure," he wrote, alluding once again to the power of blood sacrifice to unite the nation. "To Hillary Clinton, he is a tool to be used to divide people."[40] In describing Khizr Khan as Clinton's pawn, Hurt dismissed Khan's agency and free will and adopted a patronizing attitude toward the Khan family.

While such criticism spoke only to Trump's partisans, Hurt opened up another line of attack more likely to score points with antiwar voters, including those who had voted for Senator Bernie Sanders in the Democratic Party primaries. "Perhaps a better testimony from Khizr Khan," Hurt proclaimed, "would have been for him to talk about how Hillary Clinton was in the U.S. Senate when she voted to invade Iraq." Hurt rightly pointed to Hillary Clinton's vote for the Iraq War in 2003 as perhaps the most important vote of her political career. It made her vulnerable in the 2008 campaign for the US presidency, and her main rival, then-senator Barack Obama, received support from many Democrats precisely because he had been against what eventually became an unpopular war. "It was her vote," wrote Hurt, "that sent Capt. Khan to his death."

However hyperbolic, Hurt's rhetoric identified the most important aspect of Hillary Clinton's inclusion of Humayun Khan in the myth of the American blood sacrifice. The nation *had* sent Khan to his death. But the Khan family demanded no apology. Instead, they sought public recognition of the sacrifice so that Muslims could be included in the body politic. Khan's death was sad, but for Hillary Clinton it was not a tragedy. It sustained the national faith. In fact, as US secretary of state under President Obama, she continued to advocate for American leadership, a euphemism for American exceptionalism and US military intervention. She was one of the architects of the violent overthrow of Libyan dictator Mu'amar Qaddafi, and Clinton urged Obama to intervene more forcefully in the Syrian civil war to aid the rebels who were fighting both Bashar al-Assad and Da'ish, or the Islamic State. The fact that she was a female secretary of state added even more political significance to her advocacy of aggressive military interventions, as she performed a feminist valorization of the military.[41]

Clinton also echoed the liberal claims of post–Cold War presidents who went to war with Muslims that they did not wish to wage war against Islamic religion itself. Shortly after the 9/11 attacks, for example, President George W. Bush reenacted the 1957 visit of President Eisenhower to the Islamic Center in Washington, DC, in order to communicate that message. As Muslims were physically attacked and harassed in the wake of 9/11, Bush sought to restate the bargain that Eisenhower had originally struck with Muslims who were willing to support the liberal ideals of America. He drew a sharp line between terrorists and authentic Muslims, and he called on non-Muslims to recognize the contributions of Muslims to the United States: "America counts millions of Muslims amongst our citizens, and Muslims make an incredibly valuable contribution to our country," Bush said. "Muslims are doctors, lawyers, law professors, members of the military, entrepreneurs, shopkeepers, moms and dads. And they need to be treated with respect."[42]

As many scholars have documented, however, there was a wide gulf between this rhetoric of inclusion and the ways in which the administrative policies of Bush and then Obama targeted Muslims as potential terrorists. Programs and policies that stigmatized Muslims without any evidence of wrongdoing ranged from massive counterintelligence operations and the Countering Violent Extremism program to proxy denaturalization, the National Security Entry-Exit Registration System, the detention facility at Guantanamo Bay, and drone strikes.[43] Hillary Clinton was a champion of most of these policies, as Muslim Americans themselves were aware. Her strong opposition to the BDS movement (to boycott, divest from, and sanction Israel for its violations of Palestinian human rights) also alienated some Muslim voters. But in the end, Donald Trump's explicit anti-Muslim prejudices made most Muslim Americans feel as if they had little choice: according to one exit poll, 74 percent of them voted for Clinton while 13 percent voted for Trump.[44]

As the 2016 campaign transitioned from the summer convention to the fall debates, an increasing number of Muslim American critics called out Hillary Clinton for seeing Muslims only in light of their value to national security. In all three debates, Clinton framed Muslim Americans as "our eyes and ears on our front lines," leading writer Ismat Sarah Mangla to declare that "her framing of Muslims solely in terms of national security has an insidious effect in continuing to stigmatize them as something less than fully American." In the third debate, Clinton and Trump were asked about physical attacks on Muslims and other hate crimes. Trump responded by cautioning against political correctness in dealing with terrorism, which rearticulated his essential vision of the Muslim as terrorist, while Clinton once again said that Muslim Americans were on the front lines of fighting the war on terror. Activist Linda Sarsour tweeted that she was "tired of hearing how Muslims [a]r[e] only on front lines of fighting terrorism. What about front lines on immigrant rights, #BlackLivesMatter?" Writer Hussein Rashid was even more pointed: "@Hillary Clinton makes Muslims conditional citizens in America, It's standard GOP line. It would be nice to not be your toys." One of the funniest responses came from *St. Louis Post-Dispatch* columnist Aisha Sultan: "It's weird how politicians keep telling me I'm on the front line of fighting terrorism when I'm just trying to get through a sugar detox."[45]

This sarcasm and the more sober criticisms exposed the limits of Hillary Clinton's mythmaking. But Clinton continued to put the Khans' story at the center of her campaign. In the final three weeks before the election, the campaign ran an emotional minute-long ad in seven battleground states that featured Khizr Khan. In the ad, Khan tells the story of his son's sacrifice. He looks wistfully at pictures of his son in uniform. He tells the audience that his son was a Muslim American. The ad then shows Donald Trump on the stump, and Khizr Khan says that he has a question for Mr. Trump. With tears in his eyes, he asks, "Would my son have a place in your America?"[46]

Competing Myths of US Political Belonging

After Trump's surprise victory in November and his three subsequent executive orders attempting to prevent Muslim visitors and refugees from entering the nation, it became clear that the mythic Humayun Khan would not have a place in Trump's America. As powerful as the myth of the fallen Muslim American soldier was for Americans who shared tears with Khan's father, the older myth of the Muslim beast, the unassimilable foreigner, would not be replaced in narratives of US communal formation. Rather, Muslims would be kept out of the nation through both mythmaking and policymaking.

Scholars of religion and violence have offered several theories for why the myth of blood sacrifice fails to unify a country.[47] Attempts to make myths around the fallen Muslim soldier—whether Humayun Khan or Kareem Khan or all those Muslims who have fallen in service to the US since the Revolutionary War—have gained in popularity since 9/11 but have not established the authoritative multicultural liberal consensus touted by Colin Powell and Hillary Clinton. Because the country is at war in Muslim lands, and because half the country believes it is at war with Islamic religion, this myth, as appealing as it may be, is not powerful enough to overshadow the myth of the Muslim beast.[48]

Moreover, even as the liberal myth of incorporation seeks to uplift the sacrifice of Muslim Americans for the nation, it simultaneously casts Muslims as useful to the nation precisely because they come from and are intimately connected to the nation's foreign enemies. As Aziz Rana points out, this "national security citizenship . . . [is] one of the most common mechanisms for outsider groups to gain inclusion in U.S. life."[49] The problem is that the domestication of these particular Muslim bodies—the "good" Muslims—ultimately flaunts the values of American lives over the lives of Muslim "others" and, in so doing, militates against full inclusion in America. The "most fundamental binary of all—between 'us' and 'them' is hardened," writes American studies scholar Zareena Grewal. "As the Other that intrudes in our midst, the figure of the immigrant Muslim as a perpetual foreigner indexes and underscores the ontological distance between the United States and the distant, backward, pathological Muslim World from which he came."[50] In a similar vein, religious studies scholar Sylvester Johnson has argued that Muslims are often considered "perpetually, ineluctably alien" to the nation-state. They "are treated as incapable of truly belonging to the state. In the eyes of that state, neither the passage of time nor the adoption of new cultural forms alters this alien status."[51]

The war on terror extends the logic of the racial exclusion abroad, as potential terrorists are hunted down before they have a chance to attack the homeland. As many proponents of US wars in Afghanistan and Iraq argued, "It's better to fight them over there than fight them here." Despite the US government's stated policy that such wars targeted terrorist organizations and political despots, many Americans experienced these wars as struggles against whole populations of racial others, of potential monsters.

Confronting the myth of Muslim monsters has the potential to dislodge the race thinking that justifies such policies. But it is difficult to see how citizens can look beyond or question this myth if the current war on terror both at home and abroad continues in its current form. "So long as the U.S. racial state operates as the guarantor of colonial governance over predominantly Muslim polities while these are rendered as antithetical to European Christian civilization (the West)," argues Sylvester Johnson, "Islam will remain racialized as an alien subjectivity in a White settler state."[52] Without some radical reshaping of US foreign policy in the twenty-first century, Muslims are likely to continue to serve, often against their own wishes, as symbols in, on, and through which the nation is contested and created. For some, the detention, surveillance, torture, and mass killing of Muslim bodies is a necessary price paid for American empire. For other Americans, the political and economic and moral costs of global dominance are too high. But in either case, since the nation remains a primary way communities are formed in the contemporary world, sacrificing one's blood in battle for one's country will likely continue to be narrated in mythic ways.

Such mythologizing is not itself immoral. Making myths is a social process that has long been part of the human experience, and it is unlikely to recede in importance. But in the case of the myth of the fallen Muslim soldier, what policies does such mythmaking inspire and justify? Who benefits and who suffers? In the twenty-first century, the victims of direct US military invasion and covert military operations often happen to be Muslim. Their suffering ultimately redounds to Muslim

Americans—even those who support the war-making. The liberal bargain offered by Democratic politicians fails even the most patriotic Muslim Americans.

US wars conducted in the name of protecting freedom may recognize heroic Muslim sacrifices but they also work to deny freedom to Muslims both at home and abroad. The second-class citizenship of Muslim Americans in the post-9/11 era has meant, in practice, that liberal rights afforded to first-class American citizens—protection from illegal search and seizure, trial by jury and the right to confront one's accuser in a court of law, freedom of assembly and speech, equal protection under the law—could be and were suspended in the interest of the nation's security. In practice, the "nation" was not big enough to include all its people. It actually only included "real" Americans—as some politicians put it—that is, the ruling racial class.

No matter how much blood is spilled on behalf of this crooked liberal bargain offered to Muslim Americans, it cannot save them. Given the persistence of white supremacy and US imperialism, the only practical solution is to demand change through organized political dissent. Some Muslim Americans are offering the kind of resistance that has the potential to establish a more genuine American democracy, and I now turn to that dissent in the book's conclusion.

Conclusion

"The Jewish question was fundamental for politics and philosophy in the Enlightenment," asserts political scientist Anne Norton. "In our time, as the Enlightenment fades, the Muslim question has taken its place." In *On the Muslim Question*, Norton outlines the many parallels between the nineteenth- and early-twentieth-century European "Jewish question" and the contemporary European and American "Muslim question." Norton points out how, in the past, "Jews were marked out as a political threat even as they were subject to political assaults; marked as evil as conduct toward them testified to the failure of the ethical systems that had abandoned them." In a similar fashion, she asserts, now "Islam is marked as the preeminent danger to politics, to Christians, Jews, and secular humanities; to women, sex, and sexuality, and the values and institutions of the Enlightenment."[1] Norton is not the only scholar to note the parallels. Sociologist Abdolmohammad Kazemipur asserts that contemporary Western thinking regarding Muslim assimilation is rooted at least in part in nineteenth-century European and American theories about the assimilation of Eastern European Jews into Western nations. Echoing theories that constructed Jewish people as threatening and criminal due to their different religion, culture, and politics, he claims, today's popular opposition to Muslim immigrants assumes that there is a fundamental clash of civilizations or cultures between Islam and the West.[2]

The Muslim question has special meaning for the United States, whose sacred texts, including the Bill of Rights, see the curtailment of state power and the enshrining of individual rights as the destiny of human civilization. "Though we maintain our belief that law is neutral, that the Constitution secures rights, and that America has true freedom of religion," declares Norton, "American citizenship has not protected America's Muslim citizens from surveillance, detention, unlawful searches, and the assaults of discrimination."[3] This book has asserted that the Muslim question is really the American question: Will the United States abandon white supremacy both at home and abroad? Will the American nation-state define its security and well-being so that it no longer rests on a foundation of racism and global military domination? Answering the challenges posed by "the Muslim question" necessitates addressing the key policy orientations of contemporary American political life. The rights of citizenship are defined in the context of those politics, and so the fate of Muslim political participation and the future of American democracy are now one and the same.

To become truly democratic, the liberal belief in America's special mission to make the world safe for democracy via racist, imperial military intervention will have to be rejected. Liberalism can no longer be defined in contradistinction to Muslim people and their supposedly illiberal cultures. Freedom and democracy can no longer be defended by killing or imprisoning in the name of protecting "the people"—a terrible euphemism for the ruling racial class. A political revolution is needed to addresses the Muslim question as part of a broader transition to real democracy. And if this cannot be achieved, the best that many Muslims might hope for is something akin to what members of the Nation of Islam achieved in the 1950s and 1960s. They thought that such a revolution was unlikely, deciding to establish separate institutions that challenged the ideological basis of white supremacy, including both racism and colonialism, without mounting any physical attacks on the machinery of the state or its citizens. They waited on an apocalypse to kill the whiteness in human beings.

For those who wish to change American democracy, the model of El-Hajj Malik El-Shabazz, Malcolm X, offers a different path. Impatient for the day of judgement, he sought to make a Dark World political alliance that would overwhelm white domination. He unapologetically and bravely confronted what he called the hypocritical claims of American liberals even though he was being pursued by enemies of all sorts—

the US government and some African American Muslim defenders of Elijah Muhammad alike. His voice was silenced. But real freedom and democracy for all is likely impossible in the contemporary United States unless safe, public space is made for serious engagement with critics and dissenters such as Malcolm X.

The odds against a grassroots and broad-based politics of resistance against US empire are great not only because a significant percentage of the population enthusiastically supports war-making against Muslims but also because so many American liberals believe that their livelihood and their well-being are ultimately tied to maintaining US military hegemony and protecting the American homeland against "radicalism" and "extremism." As Asian American studies scholar Sunaina Maira claims, "White American liberals have an often unspoken identification with the imperial project of their nation . . . as do liberals from minority or immigrant communities who wish to assert their cultural citizenship or who (want to) believe in the notion of liberal citizenship and individual freedom in the United States."[4] Such complicity with or silent acquiescence to the state's imperialism and the tyranny required to achieve it—the violation of the state's most fundamental ethical principles as articulated in the Bill of Rights—not only harms Muslims but threatens the legitimacy of the republic too.

Dissent is the most practical strategy for those who dream of democratic change within the current structures of government. According to Maira, dissent "still engages with the role and responsibility of the nation-state and the question of belonging and rights for subjects, however marginalized."[5] Dissent can even be a form of complicity with the state when it does not challenge the fundamental injustice of the state or is appropriated and domesticated.[6] But dissent can also inspire real change via conventional means of peaceful assembly, lobbying, electoral politics, lawsuits, and so on. At other times, dissent must take a more active form of resistance, like that outlined by Martin Luther King Jr. in the 1963 "Letter from a Birmingham Jail"; its tactics might include economic boycotts, work stoppages, and sit-ins.

Some Muslims Americans have been using these tactics of dissent since 9/11. Linda Sarsour's rising prominence shows how one such Muslim American voice of dissent can gain national attention. Sarsour is not universally liked—even by other Muslim Americans—and the point in recounting her story is not to endorse her. Rather, Linda Sarsour's story shows how a dissenting Muslim American leader can work with other antiracists to oppose war-making and the national security state as a grassroots organizer and conventional political operative. Her story reveals the persistence of discrimination against voices of dissent not only by extremist Islamophobes but by mainstream liberals as well. But it suggests how engagement with Muslim American political activists offers an alternative to a liberalism mired in racism and colonialism.

Born in 1980 to Palestinian Muslim parents in New York, Sarsour has been dubbed a "Brooklyn Homegirl in a Hijab" by the *New York Times*. She was raised in the Sunset Park neighborhood of Brooklyn, and her personal style—her swagger—has been compared to that of another Brooklynite activist, the actress Rosie Perez. Sarsour married at the age of seventeen and gave birth to her first child at nineteen. She studied at Kingsborough Community College and Brooklyn College, and worked for the Arab American Association of New York, where she advocated for the victims of the law enforcement roundups of Arabs and Muslims in the days after 9/11. Later, as leader of that group, she became part of Communities United for Police Reform, partnering with the New York Civil Liberties Union and the Legal Aid Society to pass legislation reforming the New York City Police Department's racial and religious profiling and surveillance programs.[7]

From her base as a grassroots activist in New York City, Sarsour developed a national following in the decade after 9/11 and cultivated political alliances with left-leaning non-Muslim organizations and activists. She used these connections to build Muslim support for what would eventually become the Black Lives Matter movement. In 2014, when Michael Brown was killed by a police officer in Ferguson, Missouri, Sarsour telephoned Mustafa Abdullah, who worked for the American Civil Liberties Union in the Saint Louis area, and asked him, "Where is the Muslim community on this?" Abdullah credits Sarsour with inspiring him to help organize a Muslims for Ferguson group.[8] Sarsour also continued to advocate on behalf of Muslim concerns. In 2015, as part of a New York group called Coalition for Muslim School Holidays, she celebrated New York City mayor Bill de Blasio's decision to make Eid al-Fitr and Eid al-Adha official public school holidays.[9] No one stood closer to de Blasio than Sarsour as the mayor announced the policy at a press conference.[10]

While working closely with New York City Democrats, however, she was also squarely opposed to many of Democratic president Barack Obama's policies regarding Muslims. It was thus a surprise to some liberals and others when, in 2011, President Obama recognized Sarsour as a "champion of change," noting her role as "Advocacy and Civic Engagement Coordinator for the National Network for Arab American Communities (NNAAC), a network of 22 Arab American organizations in 11 states."[11] A headline in *Politico*, for example, proclaimed that "a Brooklyn Democrat who called Obama 'terrible' on civil rights will be honored by the White House." When asked how she could accept such an award while voicing criticism of the Obama administration on issues related to civil rights and immigration, Sarsour said that "my community deserves it and it's a slap in the face for Islamophobes." She also claimed that other award winners had voiced similar criticisms of the government and that it was part of the American tradition to do so. Sarsour credited Obama with trying to pass the DREAM Act, which would have prevented the deportation of immigrants who were brought to the United States when they were children, but said that she would continue to be a critic when warranted.[12]

And that is exactly what she did. Writing in the *Guardian* with activist Deepa Iyer a few years later, Sarsour contended that the Department of Homeland Security's Countering Violent Extremism program wrongly targeted Muslim Americans rather than right-wing white supremacist groups. The program would do more harm than good, the authors claimed, because it framed Muslims as potential terrorists, would lead

to more anti-Muslim discrimination, and contributed to mistrust between Muslim communities and the government.[13] On both her Twitter
feed and her Facebook page, which have been followed by hundreds of
thousands of people, Sarsour also criticized the Obama administration's
use of drones in the war on terror, its use of secret evidence to prosecute
alleged terrorists, and its profiling of Muslims without legitimate suspicion of guilt.[14]

Sarsour's star rose quickly both during and immediately after the
presidential election of 2016. She endorsed Vermont senator Bernie
Sanders for president and on April 14 gave an enthusiastic, if customary
campaign speech at a Washington Square Park rally outlining Sanders's
support of labor unions, women, immigrants, and Black Lives Matter.[15]
That same year, Sarsour worked with other Muslim activists to establish
a group called MPower, whose goal is to become the "largest Muslim-
led social and racial justice organization in the United States."[16] Then,
after Donald Trump was elected, Sarsour became cochair of the Wom-
en's March on Washington. This is the event that catapulted her into
the national limelight, as she appeared on numerous national television
shows, in magazines, and in other media. Approximately half a million
people attended the march—with millions more marching in solidarity across the United States—as Sarsour declared: "You can count on
me, your Palestinian Muslim sister, to keep her voice loud, keep her feet
on the streets, keep my head held high, because I am not afraid."[17] She
argued that the experience of Muslim Americans had presaged many of
newly elected President Trump's policies toward marginalized populations. "Many of our communities, including my community, the Muslim
community, ha[ve] been suffering in silence under the Bush administration and under the Obama administration. The very things that you are
outraged by during the election season—the Muslim registry program,
the banning of the Muslims, the dehumanization of the community
that I come from—that has been our reality for the past fifteen years."
Sarsour asserted that the connection between the Muslim question and
the fate of American democracy was now clear. She also articulated an

intersectional politics of solidarity with others, including Black women, LGBTQI women, undocumented women, women with disabilities, and all women who gave their own money rather than seeking corporate sponsorship for the Women's March.[18]

Of all her political positions, it is Sarsour's support for the boycott of, divestment from, and imposition of sanctions against the government of Israel that generates the most opposition among American liberals. The Boycott, Divestment, and Sanctions (BDS) movement, which is modeled after the anti-apartheid movement's boycott of South Africa, has three goals: to end the Israeli colonization of the West Bank (and blockade of Gaza), to recognize the "fundamental rights of the Arab-Palestinian citizens of Israel to full equality," and to allow Palestinian refugees from the 1948 Arab-Israeli war to return to their homes.[19] The BDS movement is opposed by the leadership of both the Republican and Democratic parties, several state governments, and many evangelical Christians and Jews. But the movement commands significant support in Europe, Africa, Asia, and Latin America, and its popularity has grown among younger liberals in the United States since its establishment in 2005. Israel's government and its allies in the United States see the BDS movement as a primary threat to Israel's existence, even though it is nonviolent—perhaps *because* it is nonviolent. And some of its opponents accuse the BDS movement of being inherently anti-Semitic.[20]

Opposition to Palestinian liberation movements has a long history in the United States, and, like other prominent advocates of Palestinian self-determination, Linda Sarsour has endured multiple death threats. Because Sarsour also wears a head scarf, is a woman, supports certain Democratic candidates, and proudly extols the virtues of her religion, it is not always clear whether the threats that she receives are the result of her Palestinian advocacy or her other identities and commitments. Muslim women who advocate for Palestinian freedom have been particularly vulnerable to threats of sexual violence.[21] Around the time that Sarsour was scheduled to give a commencement speech to approximately one hundred graduates at the City University School of Public Health, she received messages saying that "a good Arab is a dead Arab," "you're getting two bullets in your head," and "your time is coming." Such threats increased after some activists and politicians decided to mount organized opposition to the speech. For example, Democratic New York State Assembly member Dov Hikind released a letter from one hundred Holocaust survivors that opposed the speech and claimed that Sarsour supported Palestinian terrorists. Sarsour responded by saying that she had not planned on speaking about Israel. A number of progressive Jewish leaders defended her; 130 wrote an open letter in support. Brooklyn City Council member Brad Lander said that Sarsour was a friend of his rabbi.[22]

Sarsour's June 1 speech called on CUNY public health graduates to make "the decision never to be bystanders." Sarsour began with the story of train commuters in Portland, Oregon, who defended two women—one wearing a head scarf—against a barrage of racist slurs from an anti-Semitic neo-Nazi. Taliesin Myrddin Namkai Meche, Ricky Best, and Micah Fletcher—three white men—were stabbed by the man when they tried to calm him down. Meche, a 2006 graduate of Reed College, and Best, a US Army veteran, died as a result of their wounds. Their courage, said Sarsour, "restored a small empty space in my heart with a sense of hope." She also asked her audience to "commit to never being bystanders to poverty, lack of jobs and healthcare, sexism, violence, discrimination, racism, xenophobia, Islamophobia, anti-Semitism, and homophobia." Public health professionals, she told them, play an essential role in creating "healthy communities" that are composed of people who nurture their "mental, emotional, and physical well-being." Sarsour asked her audience to protect one another, to remain "righteously outraged" at injustice and violence, and to realize that "we are in this together."[23] It was a speech with which many Americans, of various political stripes but especially liberals, could identify.

But loud, public criticism kept coming, and Sarsour refused to compromise her message. Indeed, she used the opportunity to model an unapologetic response to the challenges facing the Muslim American community. In a July 2017 speech to the Islamic Society of North America (ISNA) annual convention, Sarsour reminded her audience of the Islamic obligation to wage jihad, or struggle, against oppression. Once, when the Prophet Muhammad was asked about the best form of jihad, Sarsour said, his response was that "a word of truth in front of a tyrant ruler or leader, that is the best form of jihad." She thus called on Muslims to follow the prophetic example and to struggle "against tyrants and rulers not only abroad in the Middle East or on the other side of the world, but here in these United States of America, where you have fascists and white supremacists and Islamophobes reigning in the White House." Conservative media reports reported that Sarsour advocated a jihad against the president, and some Twitter users circulated the idea that she should be added to a terrorist watch list. Several Muslim and Arab American community leaders rushed to defend Sarsour, some tweeting #IStandWithLinda, while various mainstream media outlets tried to explain what she meant by using the word "jihad." The *Washington Post*, for example, informed its readers that "most Muslims use it [jihad] to refer to a personal, spiritual effort to follow God, live out one's faith and strive to be a better person." Sarsour told the paper that she should "not be criminalized for being a Muslim in America. . . . I'm not going to limit who I am and how I speak because people are ignorant and racist."

Throughout 2017, Sarsour faced attacks not only from conservatives but also from liberals. After the Women's March, journalist Emma-Kate Symons wrote in *Women in the World* that Sarsour "is a religiously conservative Muslim veiled woman, embracing a fundamentalist worldview requiring women to 'modestly' cover themselves, a view which has little to do with female equality." She called Sarsour a hypocrite for supporting an "illiberal ideology that many Muslim women say is all about men controlling their bodies." Using explicitly racist language associating Sarour with terrorism, Symons said that the organizers had hijacked feminism.[24] *New York Times* staff opinion editor Bari Weiss wrote in the summer that Sarsour, like the other organizers of the Women's March, were guilty of "embracing terrorists, disdaining independent feminist voices, hating on democracies, and celebrating dictatorships."[25] She declared that the organizers "embraced decidedly illiberal causes and cultivated a radical tenor that seems to alienate the most woke." Weiss also declared that Sarsour was an anti-Zionist—that is, an opponent of the movement to establish and now sustain a Jewish national homeland in Palestine. (Perhaps needless to say, it is hardly surprising for a Palestinian to be anti-Zionist.)

As Gaby del Valle pointed out in *The Outline*, "The anti-Sarsour campaign is about more than Linda Sarsour." It was instead an attack on the feminist leadership of women of color and their privileging of intersectional social justice. For liberal critics such as Bari Weiss and *Bustle* politics editor Emily Shire, the identity politics of the Women's March was illiberal, an example of "intersectionality having gone too far."[26] Their iteration of liberal feminism is remarkably similar to the imperial feminism that, as explained in chapter 4, was at the heart of the propaganda that framed a military invasion as an opportunity to save Afghan women from Afghan men.

Responding to Weiss's op-ed and other criticism, Sarsour took to social media to proclaim:

> For the record, I am still unapologetically Muslim American, Palestinian American every single day. I will not be harassed, intimidated, bullied, smeared and/or threatened in to changing my convictions and things I hold dear to me. I know there are consequences to being fully who I am and that holding on to my lineage as a Palestinian & my unshakeable support for Palestinian liberation and my deep commitment to my religious faith can cost me a lot. It is worth it, every single second of it. We will take all necessary precautions, but we stay the path. There's gonna be moments where we have to make important decisions and I have made mine. I am part of a new generation that has carried on the legacy of activists before us—intentionally misunderstood, vilified, demonized and it didn't stop them then and won't stop us now. We are on the right side of history, only time will tell.

She also reiterated her criticism of Israeli "military occupation, colonization, and land grabbing" and reaffirmed her commitment to "Black
Lives Matter and 'Refugees Are Welcome' and 'our bodies, our choice,'
'Healthcare for all,' 'stop all wars,' and 'stand with oppressed people all
over the world.'"[27]

The attempts to silence or discredit Linda Sarsour are all the more important for the future of American democracy because, contrary to the
lies about her goals and tactics, Sarsour is no violent revolutionary. She
is a dissenter still entangled in and engaged with conventional mechanisms of US political participation. She is also an avowed American patriot. "I truly believe that dissent is the highest form of patriotism," she
told the CUNY's public health graduates. A cynic might claim that her
patriotism is instrumental, a means to an end, a way of convincing her
audience that she is not that threatening after all. But this viewpoint
ignores her long-standing pattern of appealing to American exceptionalism, a myth deeply rooted in Muslim/America. Kristin McLaren
documents how Sarsour, like other Muslim Americans, offers a Muslim
version of the American jeremiad, the venerable American rhetorical
tradition that criticizes Americans when they fail to fulfill their destiny
as a chosen people who have a special mission to perform on behalf
of the entire world. Sarsour's American jeremiad, like others, warns of
terrible consequences if things are allowed to stay as they are and offers
hope of redemption if change is accomplished. In 2015, for example, she
wrote that she believed "in the true potential of my country to be the
greatest nation in the world and every day I push my government to
live up to its ideals." Donald Trump's popularity, according to Sarsour,
is a "reflection of what has been acceptable for far too long." And: "He is
a symptom of the diseases and political exclusion in America," and the
"hate, racism & xenophobia [that Trump encourages] can be deadly."[28]

In his 1978 classic, *American Jeremiad*, Sacvan Bercovitch noted that
dissent operating within acceptable cultural and political boundaries
could sustain the political status quo, acting as a steam valve to release
the pressure of oppression and injustice. He "warned that the Ameri-

can jeremiad too readily becomes absorbed into a self-congratulatory celebration of American progress." For McLaren, however, Sarsour's exceptionalist rhetoric, like that of the post-1966 Martin Luther King Jr., manages to avoid such traps: "This American hijabi jeremiad provides a radical critique of the national consensus, and while it celebrates moments of progress, has resisted complete absorption into self-congratulation."[29] Moreover, Sarsour's resistance goes beyond rhetorical critique as she has engaged in nonviolent direct action. For instance, in March 2018, as she protested the US Congress's refusal to take action on the Deferred Action for Childhood Arrivals, or DACA Act, which protects children who were brought to the United States illegally, Sarsour was arrested alongside Muslim American leaders, including Nihad Awad, Zahra Billoo, Omar Sulieman, and Dawud Walid, outside the office of Speaker of the House Paul Ryan.[30]

As Sunaina Maira reminds us, even acts of civil disobedience can be complicit in supporting the basic structures of the US. nation-state. Sarsour's goals may be oriented toward radical policy changes in the US government and even structural changes in the US and global economies, but they do not challenge the global political order of nation-states. As much as she embraces the legacy of Malcolm X, whom she frequently quotes, she is not advocating any sort of violent resistance to the US nation-state or to nation-states more generally. Like Sarsour, Malcolm X was a New York–based activist who believed in the power of grassroots religious and political institution-building, and at the end of his life he sought allies of color across the political spectrum both at home and abroad. He also saw Islamic religion as consonant with liberal ideas of freedom and criticized liberal institutions for their selective protection of some people's liberty over that of others. But unlike Sarsour, Malcolm X did not rehearse the rhetoric of American patriotism, instead choosing to expose the hypocrisy of national myths in sarcastic rather than solemn tones. Perhaps most dangerously for the American political status quo, Malcolm X warned that Black freedom in 1964 would come through the ballot or the bullet, and he publicly mused about organizing a group of freedom fighters to oppose Congo-lese leader Moise Tshombe, the U.S-backed leader who murdered Prime Minister Patrice Lumumba.[31]

For many leftists and other radicals, Linda Sarsour's vision may not be enough, although many of them work with and support her. In ar-ticulating the hope for reform—and even if her patriotic rhetoric is instrumentalist—Sarsour does not reckon explicitly with the idea that democratic, liberal states may be structurally incapable of accommodat-ing ethno-racial pluralism. As we have seen, in the election of 2016, a sig-nificant number of Muslim Americans, and other Americans, chose not to vote because of a feeling that neither major-party candidate offered the chance for real change. Some cynically, but perhaps realistically, hoped that, at the very least, Donald Trump would accelerate the destruction of the liberal status quo and perhaps the state itself, and thus set the condi-tions for something new. Some Muslim Americans also articulated more utopian and constructive visions of radical political change.[32]

This book has made the case that the fate of American democracy has been and will continue to be tied to the assimilation of Muslim Ameri-cans into the body politic—not as vanquished enemies or sacrificial lambs, but as equal partners in the making of a political community committed to justice and equity. As it is currently construed, liberal-ism makes that kind of democracy impossible. US politics since World War II has been grounded in an institutional liberalism that, while ex-isting ostensibly to spread the blessings of liberty to all, has furthered domestic racism and American empire. Muslim Americans have been among American democracy's most potent critics, and they remain its victims—surveilled, prosecuted, and terrorized. In the 1950s and 1960s, it was the Nation of Islam that provided a potent Muslim critique of American democracy's failures. The dogged repression and marginal-ization of this group by the federal government, the liberal media, and liberal academics testify to the costs of white supremacy: liberalism re-mained more focused on protecting white racial supremacy, alienating these Americans from the liberal promise of life and liberty for all.

Looking back, it seems that many liberals can now embrace the Nation of Islam's critique of American racism and the US military invasion of Vietnam. For some liberals, the radical dreams of Malcolm X that people of color might live as "free humans," as part of communities in which Black individuals could determine their collective political, economic, and cultural future, are at the least "understandable." At the end of the Cold War and especially after 9/11, however, regrets about Vietnam and empathy with or sympathy for radicals such as Malcolm X meant little as many national liberal leaders such as Hillary Clinton reacted to 9/11 using many of the strategies and much of the rhetoric from the old Cold War liberal playbook. Though other liberals raised concerns and a few Democrats protested, most politicians supported a massive expansion of government power and the expenditure of billions of dollars to reorganize the government for a long war on terror both at home and abroad. Muslim women's bodies became central to the liberal propaganda that favored US military interventionism, though Muslim American women themselves largely rejected this instrumental use of their bodies to justify the deaths of Muslims abroad. Millions of lives were lost either directly or indirectly because of US military intervention, and even though Muslim Americans were willing to die in those battles, a grossly anti-Muslim president was still elected in 2016.

Visionary Muslim American political voices, both at the grassroots and in public, once again articulated a different way, a call to abandon the empire and to cultivate a vibrant and safe public square where Americans might oppose government policies on a whole host of issues—from support of Israel to mass incarceration—without having reason to fear for their lives, their liberty, and their livelihoods. Like Malcolm X and many in the Nation of Islam, they pointed out the complicity of both liberal and conservative media, popular culture, and politicians in making America undemocratic. But such unapologetic and intersectional Muslim American political voices continue to be shunned, including by many Democrats.

On January 3, 2019, Linda Sarsour was on hand to celebrate the swearing in of the first two female Muslim members of Congress. She proudly posted photographs of herself with Somali American Rep. Ilhan Omar of Minnesota, the first member of the US House to wear a hijab. "Today was JOY. Today was PRIDE," Sarsour wrote on Facebook. "Today was full of laughter and tears. For every lil girl, especially lil girls of color—this is for you. You are our future congresswomen."[33] Sarsour's dress for the occasion was a traditional Palestinian thawb, which was also worn by fellow Muslim and Palestinian American Rashida Tlaib, newly elected to represent Michigan's 13th district. It was a glorious day for many Muslim, Arab, and Somali Americans and their allies. As one might have predicted from the treatment of Sarsour, however, threats, harassment, and condemnation soon became a daily reality for these Congresswomen. And the grief came from different political directions—from conservatives who associated Tlaib and Omar with terrorism or an Islamic takeover of America, from both Democrats and Republicans who wanted to blunt their criticism of Israel, and from the Saudi-funded *Al-Arabiya* news network, which sought to silence their opposition to Saudi Arabia's war on Yemen.[34]

Whether Rep. Omar and Rep. Tlaib will be able to weather the threats and criticism in the long term is a question important not only for their political careers but also for the republic. The future of Muslim Americans such as Reps. Omar and Tlaib is the future of US democracy. Too many Americans regard the political vision of progressives such as Linda Sarsour and Reps. Omar and Tlaib as beyond the pale of American politics, unworthy even of serious consideration, dialogue, and engagement. This is why assimilating those political voices—without muting or appropriating them—is so essential to the future of American politics. The very policies, laws, and institutions that make impossible the assimilation of Muslim Americans also make America undemocratic for many of its people. The prosecution of the war on terror both at home and abroad is a classic example not so much of American national security concerns trumping liberty but rather of American liberalism's long commitment to prioritizing the safety and security of some humans over others. Because of this war-making, Muslim Americans cannot be free, and the ethno-racial state that invests in white supremacy is sustained. Even more, human empathy for the victims of US foreign policy disappears from the public sphere as Muslim American voices are alienated, ignored, or repressed.

In the end, then, the success of Muslim American political participation speaks not only to establishing individual liberty and rights for all, but also to the possibility of a flourishing political community. Since Muslims are just 1 to 2 percent of the US population, Muslim American participation in US democracy, like that of other religious and racial minorities, requires coalitions in which interests can be linked and shared destinies can be imagined. In all its messiness, inevitable conflict, and regrettable compromise, politics can become an inclusive act of community-making and social change. But that kind of democracy will require a change in the way that both conservatives and liberals receive Muslim American voices. Most fundamentally, it will require significant change in the policies and structures that cast them out of the American political community.

ACKNOWLEDGMENTS

The scholars who anonymously review one's manuscript, for little to no money, are not often the first people who are mentioned in a book's acknowledgements, but let me change that right here: whoever you are, thank you for offering remarkably constructive and detailed recommendations for improvement. You truly helped me write a better book. Most importantly, you encouraged me to let my voice ring. Whatever shortcomings that remain are mine.

I am deeply grateful to Jeremy Rehwaldt for offering numerous suggestions that made the manuscript better. Rosemary Corbett also read the whole thing, and her incisive comments deeply shaped my thinking about the book's arguments. At New York University Press, my editor, Jennifer Hammer, gave me extensive feedback on a couple drafts, and I can't express how much I appreciate the chance to work with and learn from her. Thanks, as well, to NYU Press editor Eric Zinner and the many professionals who do such a great job at the press. I am also grateful to Dan Geist for the astute copyediting.

I shared the ideas in this book over the last decade and a half with academic and other public audiences mainly in the United States but also in the Middle East and Europe. I want to acknowledge the many institutions that created an opportunity for me to develop the work that has gone into the book. These include scholarly associations such as the American Studies Association, the American Academy of Religion, the Middle East Studies Association, and the American Historical Association. Just as important are the many schools where I gave lectures about this subject matter: the Indiana University School of Liberal Arts in Indianapolis, St. Antony's College at Oxford University, the University of Jordan, Michigan State University, University of Missouri, University of Illinois, the American University of Beirut, Georgetown University, Arizona State University, Allegheny College, Duke University, Denison University, Columbia University, Washington University, Boston University, University of Heidelberg, University of Toronto, and Stanford University.

Colleagues around the world inspired me, schooled me, and/or offered feedback on my research. Some are acknowledged in the endnotes of the book, but I also want to name some of them here. They include Su'ad Abdul Khabeer, Rebecca Alpert, Hatem Bazian, David Craig, Faisal Devji, John Esposito, Zareena Grewal, Andrew Gyory, Juliane Hammer, Kelly Hayes, Sally Howell, Andrea Jain, Sylvester Johnson, Ahmet Karamustafa, Maryam Kashani, Zaheer Kazmi, Jason Kelly, Mohammad Hassan Khalil, Missy Dehn Kubitschek, the late G. J. A. Lubbe, Melani McAlister, Aminah McCloud, Alaina Morgan, Bill Mullen, Susan Nance, Junaid Rana, Royal Rhodes, Omid Safi, Vernon Schubel, Andrew Shryock, Peter Thuesen, Richard Brent Turner, Judith Weisenfeld, and Rachel Wheeler.

Various parts of the research and writing for this book were supported financially by the Carnegie Corporation of New York, the Fulbright Program of the US Department of State, the Indiana University School of Liberal Arts, and the Institute for the Arts and Humanities at IUPUI. I am grateful for their support, but these institutions bear no responsibility for the book's content.

Some of this material has been published elsewhere. Much of chapter 2 originally appeared as "The Political Meanings of Elijah Muhammad's Nation of Islam," in *Islam after Liberalism*, edited by Faisal Devji and Zaheer Kazmi (London: Hurst, 2017), 263–80; it is reproduced here by kind permission of Hurst Publishers. Most of chapter 3 was featured in "'My Heart Is in Cairo': Malcolm X, the Arab Cold War, and the Making of Islamic Liberation Ethics," *Journal of American History* 102, no. 3 (2015): 775–98. A portion of chapter 4 was adapted from "Transnational Muslim Americans: Four Women in Jordan," *Marburg Journal of Religion* 17, no. 2 (2013): 1–18. A different version of chapter 5 appears in *Muslims and US Politics Today*, edited by Mohammad Hassan Khalil (Boston: ILEX/Harvard University Press, in press). I gratefully acknowledge all of these publishers.

NOTES

INTRODUCTION

1 George Lipsitz, *The Possessive Investment in Whiteness: How White People Profit from Identity Politics*, rev. and expanded ed. (Philadelphia: Temple University Press, 2006), 1.

2 For a different but complementary account of liberalism in Muslim America, see Rosemary R. Corbett, *Making Moderate Islam: Sufism, Service, and the "Ground Zero Mosque" Controversy* (Stanford, CA: Stanford University Press, 2017).

3 Sylvester A. Johnson, *African American Religions, 1500–2000: Colonialism, Democracy, and Freedom* (New York: Cambridge University Press, 2015); Edmund S. Morgan, *American Slavery, American Freedom: The Ordeal of Colonial Virginia* (New York: W. W. Norton, 1975); Edmund S. Morgan, *Investing the People: The Rise of Popular Sovereignty in England and America* (New York: W. W. Norton, 1988); Michael Mann, *The Dark Side of Democracy* (New York: Cambridge University Press, 2005); Michel Foucault, *Society Must Be Defended: Lectures at the Collège de France*, ed. Mauro Bertani and Alessandro Fontana (New York: Picador, 2003).

4 Robert J. Allison, *The Crescent Obscured: The United States and the Muslim World, 1776–1815* (Chicago: University of Chicago Press, 1995), 3–34.

5 Peter Gottschalk with Gabriel Greenberg, *Islamophobia and Anti-Muslim Sentiment: Picturing the Enemy*, 2d ed. (Lanham, MD: Rowman & Littlefield, 2019), 77–162.

6 See Conrad Cherry, *God's New Israel: Religious Interpretations of American Destiny*, rev. ed. (Chapel Hill: University of North Carolina Press, 1998).

7 James R. Arnold, *The Moro War: How American Battled a Muslim Insurgency in the Philippine Jungle, 1902–1913* (New York: Bloomsbury, 2011).

8 Rosemary Corbett, personal correspondence, September 13, 2018; Julian Go, "Myths of Nation and Empire: The Logic of America's Liberal Empire-State," *Thesis Eleven* 139, no. 1 (April 2017): 69–83.

9 Ta-Nehisi Coates, *We Were Eight Years in Power: An American Tragedy* (New York: One World, 2017), 64–65.

10 Johnson, *African American Religions*, 5.

11 Ibram X. Kendi, *Stamped from the Beginning: The Definitive History of Racist Ideas in America* (New York: Nation Books, 2016), 2.

12 Melvin Oliver and Thomas M. Shapiro, *Black Wealth / White Wealth: A New Perspective on Racial Inequality* (New York: Routledge, 2006).

13 Sunaina Marr Maira, *Missing: Youth, Citizenship, and Empire after 9/11* (Durham, NC: Duke University Press, 2009), 23.

14 For a critique of contemporary US military power, see, for example, David Vine, *Base Nation: How U.S. Military Bases Abroad Harm America and the World* (New York: Henry Holt, 2015).

15 For the origins of this policy, see Melvyn P. Leffler, *A Preponderance of Power: National Security, the Truman Administration, and the Cold War* (Stanford, CA: Stanford University Press, 1992).

16 Juliane Hammer, "Center Stage," in Ernst, *Islamophobia in America*, 107–44; and see Juliane Hammer, *American Muslim Women, Religious Authority, and Activism: More than a Prayer* (Austin: University of Texas Press, 2013). See also Jamillah Karim, *American Muslim Women: Negotiating Race, Class, and Gender within the Umma* (New York: New York University Press, 2008).

CHAPTER 1. THE POLITICAL ASSIMILATION OF MUSLIM AMERICANS

1 "Biography," Congressman André Carson from the 7th District of Indiana, accessed May 1, 2018, https://carson.house.gov.

2 "Rep. André Carson's 2016 Report Card," GovTrack, accessed May 1, 2018, www.govtrack.us.

3 "Issues," Congressman André Carson from the 7th District of Indiana, accessed May 1, 2018, https://carson.house.gov.

4 "Roll Call's 2018 Election Guide," Roll Call, accessed May 1, 2018, https://media.cq.com.

5 "Rep. André Carson's 2016 Report Card."

6 "Scores: House of Representatives," ProgressivePunch, accessed February 14, 2019, https://progressivepunch.org.

7 "Carson's Grandson Wants Nomination," *CongressDaily*, January 7, 2008; "Indiana: Grandson Wins House Seat," *New York Times*, March 12, 2008, www.nytimes.com.

8 "Biography," Congressman André Carson.

9 Paul Vale, "Muslim Congressman André Carson on the Bible Belt, Equal Marriage, Madrassas and an LGBT President," *Huffington Post UK*, November 21, 2014, www.huffingtonpost.co.uk.

10 Ruth Holladay, "André Carson on Identity and Belief," January 6, 2008, www.ruthholladay.com.

11 Ivan V. Natividad, "Rep. Rapper: From Rap Battles in High School Halls to Congress," *Roll Call*, January 17, 2012, www.rollcall.com.

12 Kyle Long, "Congressman Carson on Hip Hop and Politics," *Nuvo*, September 30, 2015, www.nuvo.net.

13 Nathan Guttman, "The 'Other Muslim' on Congress," *Forward*, March 16, 2011, https://forward.com.

14 "Candidate: André Carson," J Street PAC, accessed May 1, 2018, https://donate.jstreetpac.org. According to J Street, "Congressman Carson, the second Muslim

ever election [*sic*] to Congress, has been a consistent ally of the two-state solution, human rights in the Middle East and the Iran nuclear deal. Car[s]on is a reliable advocate in Congress for pro-Israel, pro-peace Americans."

15 Emmarie Huetteman, "Trumps's Words Have Added Sting for 2 Muslims in Congress," *New York Times*, December 11, 2015, A13.

16 Vale, "Muslim Congressman André Carson."

17 As of 2018, he was ranked 502nd out of 530 currently serving members by *Congressional Quarterly*, "Wealth of Congress," www.rollcall.com.

18 Amber Stearns, "(More than Just a) Muslim in the House," *Nuvo*, February 28, 2015, www.nuvo.net.

19 "Secure Freedom Dossier: Rep. André Carson's Ties to the Muslim Brotherhood," Center for Security Policy, February 6, 2015, www.centerforsecuritypolicy.org.

20 "Group Warns: Congressman with Muslim Brotherhood Ties Now on Intelligence Committee," Religious Freedom Coalition, February 25, 2015, www.religious-freedomcoalition.org. The group's defamation of Carson was accompanied by a photo of him wearing an orange-colored scarf and head covering that he wore out of respect when he visited a Sikh gurdwara—not a mosque.

21 Sam Stein and Jessica Schulberg, "Witness at Ted Cruz Hearing Accuses Congress' Two Muslim Members of Muslim Brotherhood Ties," *Huffington Post*, June 28, 2016, www.huffingtonpost.com.

22 "Views about Anti-Americanism among U.S. Muslims Have Grown More Partisan," Pew Research Center, February 2, 2016, www.pewforum.org.

23 For some debunking of these racist fantasies, see "Civilization Jihad: Debunking the Conspiracy Theory," *Bridge Initiative*, February 2, 2016, bridge.georgetown. edu; and Arnold R. Isaacs, "American Islamophobia's Fake Facts," *Tom Dispatch*, July 31, 2018, tomdispatch.com.

24 Aleksandra Sandstrom, "Faith on the Hill," Pew Research Center, January 3, 2017, www.pewforum.org.

25 Abdelkader H. Sinno, ed., *Muslims in Western Politics* (Bloomington: Indiana University Press, 2009), 85.

26 Emma Green, "How American Muslims Are Trying to Take Back Their Government," *Atlantic*, April 16, 2017, www.theatlantic.com.

27 Abigail Hauslohner, "The Blue Muslim Wave: American Muslims Launch Political Campaigns," *Washington Post*, April 15, 2018, www.washingtonpost.com.

28 Edward E. Curtis IV, "Politics," in *Encyclopedia of Muslim-American History*, ed. Edward E. Curtis IV (New York: Facts on File, 2010), 2:459–64; "Elected Muslim Officials—Federal, State, and Local Levels," *Muslim Observer*, November 20, 2008, muslimobserver.com; "The Legislator: Ilhan Omar," *Time*, September 18, 2017, www.time.com.

29 Sonja Spear, "Elias Adam Zerhouni," in Curtis, *Encyclopedia of Muslim-American History*, 2:606; Zalmay Khalilzad, *The Envoy: From Kabul to the White House, My Journey through a Turbulent World* (New York: St. Martin's, 2016); "Farah

Pandith," Council on Foreign Relations, accessed July 26, 2018, www.cfr.org; "Huma Abedin," *Politico*, n.d., accessed May 5, 2018, www.politico.com.

30 Terry Alford, *Prince among Slaves: The True Story of an African Prince Sold into Slavery in the American South*, 30th anniversary ed. (New York: Oxford University Press, 2007).

31 Edward E. Curtis IV, *Muslim Americans in the Military: Centuries of Service* (Bloomington: Indiana University Press, 2016), 17–22.

32 Omar F. Abd-Allah, *A Muslim in Victorian America: The Life of Alexander Russell Webb* (New York: Oxford University Press, 2006).

33 Edward E. Curtis IV, "United States Foreign Relations," in Curtis, *Encyclopedia of Muslim-American History*, 2:553–59.

34 Jason Springs, "Civil Religion," in *Religion and Culture: Contemporary Practices and Perspectives*, ed. Richard D. Hecht and Vincent F. Biondo III (Minneapolis: Fortress, 2012), 9.

35 Abdo A. Elkholy, *The Arab Moslems in the United States* (New Haven, CT: College and University Press, 1966); Kambiz GhaneaBassiri, *A History of Islam in America* (New York: Cambridge University Press, 2010), 228–71.

36 Curtis, "Politics."

37 "U.S. Muslims Concerned about Their Place in Society, but Continue to Believe in the American Dream," Pew Research Center, July 26, 2017, 85–87, www.pewresearch.org.

38 Dahlia Magohed and Youssef Chouhoud, *American Muslim Poll 2017: Muslims at the Crossroads* (Dearborn, MI: Institute for Social Policy and Understanding, 2017), 6, www.ispu.org.

39 Ibid.

40 Karam Dana, Bryan Wilcox Archuleta, and Matt Barreto, "The Political Incorporation of Muslims in the United States: The Mobilizing Role of Religiosity in Islam," *Journal of Race, Ethnicity, and Politics* 2, no. 2 (2017): 1–32. See also Amaney Jamal, "The Political Participation and Engagement of Muslim Americans: Mosque Involvement and Group Consciousness," *American Politics Research* 33, no. 4 (July 2005): 521–44.

41 Farida Jalalzai, "The Politics of Muslim America," *Politics and Religion* 2 (2009): 179.

42 Vale, "Muslim Congressman André Carson."

43 For historical coverage of African American Muslim and Arab American Muslim public life, see GhaneaBassiri, *History of Islam in America*; Edward E. Curtis IV, *Muslims in America: A Short History* (New York: Oxford University Press, 2009); and Curtis, *Encyclopedia of Muslim-American History*.

44 Pamela E. Pennock, *The Rise of the Arab American Left: Activists, Allies, and Their Fight against Imperialism and Racism, 1960s–1980s* (Chapel Hill: University of North Carolina Press, 2017).

45 "U.S. Muslims Concerned," 51, 94.

46 Political participation is only one sign of assimilation in a society. Sociologist
Abdelmohammad Kazemipur points out that assimilation occurs in numerous
"institutional, media, economic, and social domains." Factors used to measure
such assimilation may include "participating in the political and civic life of the
host societies, subscribing to the majority's work ethic, and taking responsibility
for one's economic life without relying on the support of the host government."
Other indices of assimilation include "obeying the law, following the host society's
dress code, keeping the neighbourhood clean, speaking the language of the host
society," and learning the history of the host country. Abdolmohammad
Kazemipur, *The Muslim Question in Canada: A Story of Segmented Integration*
(Vancouver: UBC Press, 2014), 31–32.

47 Robert L. McKenzie, "Anti-Muslim Activities in the United States," New America,
www.newamerica.org.

48 Katayoun Kishi, "Assaults against Muslims Surpass 2001 Levels," Pew Research
Center, November 15, 2017, www.pewresearch.org; see also Nathan Sandholtz,
Lynn Langton, and Michael Planty, "Hate Crime Victimization, 2003–2011," US
Department of Justice, Bureau of Justice Statistics, March 2013, www.bjs.gov.

49 Jane Stancill, "Sister of Slain UNC Student: 'Let's End the Hate,'" *Raleigh News and
Observer*, November 14, 2016, www.newsobserver.com; Margot Talbot, "The Story
of a Hate Crime," *New Yorker*, June 22, 2015, www.newyorker.com.

50 Jeff Diamant, "American Muslims Are Concerned—But Also Satisfied with Their
Lives," Pew Research Center, July 26, 2017, www.pewresearch.org.

51 "How the General Public Views Muslims and Islam," Pew Research Center, July
26, 2017, www.pewforum.org.

52 Diamant, "American Muslims Are Concerned."

53 Analysis of the institutional and structural roots of anti-Muslim racism and
xenophobia can be found in Edward W. Said, *Covering Islam: How the Media
and the Experts Determine How We See the Rest of the World*, updated ed. (New
York: Vintage Books, 1997); Junaid Rana, *Terrifying Muslims: Race and Labor in
the South Asian Diaspora* (Durham, NC: Duke University Press, 2011); Deepa
Kumar, *Islamophobia and the Politics of Empire* (Chicago: Haymarket Books,
2012); Carl W. Ernst, ed., *Islamophobia in America: The Anatomy of Intolerance*
(New York: Palgrave Macmillian, 2013); Christopher Bail, *Terrified: How
Anti-Muslim Fringe Organizations Became Mainstream* (Princeton, NJ:
Princeton University Press, 2015); Todd H. Green, *The Fear of Islam: An
Introduction to Islamophobia in the West* (Minneapolis: Fortress, 2015), Nathan
Lean, *The Islamophobia Industry: How the Right Manufactures Hatred of
Muslims*, 2nd ed. (London: Pluto, 2017); Peter Gottschalk and Gabriel
Greenberg, *Islamophobia and Anti-Muslim Sentiment: Picturing the Enemy*, 2nd
ed. (Lanham, MD: Rowman & Littlefield, 2018).

54 Council of American-Islamic Relations, *Targeted: 2018 Civil Rights Report*
(Washington, DC: CAIR, 2018), www.islamophobia.org.

55 "Anti-Muslim Discrimination," American Civil Liberties Union, accessed February 14, 2019, www.aclu.org.

56 Andrew McCabe, "Statement Before the House Appropriations Committee, Subcommittee on Commerce, Justice, Science, and Related Agencies: FBI Budget Request for Fiscal Year 2018," June 21, 2017, www.fbi.gov.

57 Jesse J. Norris and Hanna Grol-Prokopczyk, "Estimating the Prevalence of Entrapment in Post-9/11 Terrorism Cases," *Journal of Criminal Law and Criminology* 105, no. 3 (2015): 609–78.

58 Jesse J. Norris and Hanna Grol-Prokopczyk, "Temporal Trends in U.S. Counterterrorism Sting Operations, 1989–2014," *Critical Studies on Terrorism* 11, no. 2 (2018): 4.

59 Trevor Aaronson, "The Informants," *Mother Jones*, September/October 2011, www.motherjones.com; see also Trevor Aaronsen, *The Terror Factory: Inside the FBI's Manufactured War on Terrorism* (New York: Ig Publishing, 2013), 44–45.

60 Eric Lichtblau, "F.B.I. Steps Up Use of Stings in ISIS Cases," *New York Times*, June 7, 2016, www.newyorktimes.com.

61 Human Rights Watch, *Illusion of Justice: Human Rights Abuses in U.S. Terrorism Prosecutions* (New York: Human Rights Watch and Columbia University, Human Rights Institute, 2014), 3, www.hrw.org.

62 Norris and Grol-Prorkopczyk, "Temporal Trends," 12.

63 Human Rights Watch, *Illusion of Justice*, 3.

64 Norris and Grol-Prorkopczyk, "Estimating the Prevalence of Entrapment," 610.

65 Britney J. McMahan, "Brandon Mayfield," in Curtis, *Encyclopedia of Muslim-American History*, 2:363–64.

66 James Yee with Aimee Molloy, *For God and Country: Faith and Patriotism under Fire* (New York: PublicAffairs, 2005).

67 Daviel DeFraia, "Scenes from a Black Site," ProPublica, May 7, 2018, www.propublica.com.

68 Diana Coleman, "Guantanamo Bay, Cuba," in Curtis, *Encyclopedia of Muslim-American History*, 1:219–21.

CHAPTER 2. THE NATION OF ISLAM AND THE COLD WAR LIBERAL CONSENSUS

1 For an introduction to 1960s US liberalism, see Calvin Mackenzie and Robert Weisbrot, *The Liberal House: Washington and the Politics of Change in the 1960s* (New York: Penguin, 2008); and Alonzo L. Hamby, *Liberalism and Its Challengers: From F.D.R. to Bush*, 2nd ed. (New York: Oxford University Press, 1992).

2 For Blyden, see Hollis Lynch, *Edward Wilmot Blyden: Pan-Negro Patriot, 1832–1912* (London: Oxford University Press, 1967). For Dusé Ali, see Alex Lubin, *Geographies of Liberation: The Making of an Afro-Arab Political Imaginary* (Chapel Hill: University of North Carolina Press, 2014), 48–77; and Ian Duffield, "Some

American Influences on Dusé Mohammed Ali," in *Pan-African Biography*, ed. Robert A. Hill (Los Angeles: UCLA African Studies Center/Crossroads, 1987).

3　Kambiz GhaneaBassiri, *A History of Islam in America* (New York: Cambridge University Press, 2010), 165–227.

4　While questions about the Nation of Islam's legitimacy as an Islamic religious group remain a fixture of various discourses, many specialists in the study of Islam in America have argued that the Nation of Islam should be understood as part of the larger history of Islamic religion's development in the United States. See, for example, Edward E. Curtis IV, *Black Muslim Religion in the Nation of Islam, 1960–1975* (Chapel Hill: University of North Carolina Press, 2006); GhaneaBassiri, *History of Islam in America*; Zareena Grewal, *Islam Is a Foreign Country: American Muslims and the Global Crisis of Authority* (New York: New York University Press, 2014); Aminah Beverly McCloud, *African American Islam* (New York: Routledge, 1995); and Juliane Hammer and Omid Safi, eds., *Cambridge Companion to American Islam* (New York: Oxford University Press, 2013).

5　On the establishment and postwar growth of the Nation of Islam, see Claude Andrew Clegg III, *An Original Man: The Life and Times of Elijah Muhammad* (New York: St. Martin's, 1997); Curtis, *Black Muslim Religion*; E. U. Essien-Udom, *Black Nationalism: A Search for an Identity in America* (Chicago: University of Chicago Press, 1962); Mattias Gardell, *In the Name of Elijah Muhammad: Louis Farrakhan and the Final Call* (Durham, NC: Duke University Press, 1996); and C. Eric Lincoln, *The Black Muslims in America*, 3rd. ed. (Grand Rapids, MI: Eerdmans, 1994).

6　Curtis, *Black Muslim Religion*, 127–30.

7　Clegg, *Original Man*, 135–36, 189.

8　*Chicago Daily Defender*, October 3, 1959; Lincoln, *Black Muslims in America*, 143.

9　Karl Evanzz, "The FBI and the Nation of Islam," in *The FBI and Religion: Faith and National Security before and after 9/11*, ed. Sylvester A. Johnson and Steven Weitzman (Berkeley: University of California Press, 2017), 148–67.

10　Robert A. Hill, *The FBI's RACON: Racial Conditions in the United States* (Boston: Northeastern, 1995), 4.

11　Ernest Allen Jr., "When Japan Was 'Champion of the Darker Races': Satokata Takahashi and the Flowering of Black Messianic Nationalism," *Black Scholar* 24 (Winter 1994): 23–46. See also Keisha N. Blain, *Set the World on Fire: Black Nationalist Women and the Global Struggle for Freedom* (Philadelphia: University of Pennsylvania Press, 2018).

12　Clegg, *Original Man*, 70, 72–73, 82, 90–91, 172, 181, 182, 187, 283.

13　Edward E. Curtis IV, *Muslim Americans in the Military: Centuries of Service* (Bloomington: Indiana University Press, 2016), 27–32.

14　GhaneaBassiri, *History of Islam in America*, 238–41, 258–59.

15 Dwight D. Eisenhower, Remarks at Islamic Center, June 28, 1957, http://www.presidency.ucsb.edu.

16 Penny Von Eschen, *Race against Empire: Black Americans and Anticolonialism, 1937–1957* (Ithaca, NY: Cornell University Press, 1997), 174.

17 Mattias Gardell, *In the Name of Elijah Muhammad: Minister Louis Farrakhan and the Final Call* (Durham, NC: Duke University Press, 1996), 72–76; Sean McCloud, *Making the American Religious Fringe: Exotics, Subversives, and Journalists, 1955–1993* (Chapel Hill: University of North Carolina Press, 2004), 55–95.

18 Robert A. Caro, *The Years of Lyndon Johnson: Master of the Senate* (New York: Knopf, 2002); Robert A. Caro, *The Years of Lyndon Johnson: The Passage to Power* (New York: Knopf, 2012).

19 Curtis, *Black Muslim Religion*, 36.

20 Federal policy on housing is an excellent case in point, as George Lipsitz outlines. The Federal Housing Act of 1934, part of President Franklin Roosevelt's New Deal, provided federal financial support toward the expansion of credit for the purchase of homes—but Federal Housing Administration (FHA) policies directed almost all of this new home financing toward building all-white suburbs. Between 1934 and 1962, less than 2 percent of the $120 billion home financing guaranteed by the FHA and the Veterans Administration (now called the Department of Veterans Affairs) went to families of color. It is hardly surprising, given the disinvestment in urban housing, that by the 1970s various urban renewal projects targeted sixteen hundred Black neighborhoods for demolition. The 1964 Civil Rights Act did not fix the problem. Instead, it granted an exemption to antidiscrimination regulations for federal mortgage insurance programs. The 1968 Fair Housing Act then outlawed racial discrimination in lending policies, but it did not grant the Department of Housing and Urban Development (HUD) any effective enforcement powers. George Lipsitz, *The Possessive Investment in Whiteness: How White People Profit from Identity Politics*, rev. ed. (Philadelphia: Temple University Press, 2006), 29. See also Kenneth Jackson, *Crabgrass Frontier: The Suburbanization of the United States* (New York: Oxford University Press, 1985); Douglas S. Massey and Nancy A. Denton, *American Apartheid: Segregation and the Making of the Underclass* (Cambridge, MA: Harvard University Press, 1993); and Mindy Thompson Fullilove, *Root Shock: How Tearing Up City Neighborhoods Hurts America, and What We Can Do about It* (New York: Ballantine Books, 2004).

21 Lipsitz, *Possessive Investment in Whiteness*, 5–7.

22 William L. Van DeBurg, *New Day in Babylon: The Black Power Movement and American Culture, 1965–1975* (Chicago: University of Chicago Press, 1992).

23 Frank T. Donner, *The Age of Surveillance: The Aims and Methods of America's Political Intelligence System* (New York: Knopf, 1981), 178, 212–13.

24 Curtis, *Black Muslim Religion*, 4–5, 35–65.

25 See Edward E. Curtis IV, ed., *Columbia Sourcebook of Muslims in the United States* (New York: Columbia University Press, 2008), 18–22, 53–58; A. J. Toynbee, *Civilization on Trial* (New York: Oxford University Press, 1948), 205; and Edward E. Curtis IV, "Islamism and Its African American Muslim Critics: Black Muslims in the Era of the Arab Cold War," *American Quarterly* 59, no. 3 (2007): 695–96.

26 Curtis, "Islamism and Its African American Muslim Critics," 683–709.

27 For an account that traces the remaking of American religions along conservative and liberal political lines, see Robert Wuthnow, *The Restructuring of American Religion: Society and Faith since World War II* (Princeton, NJ: Princeton University Press, 1988).

28 Edward E. Curtis IV, "Islamizing the Black Body: Ritual and Power in Elijah Muhammad's Nation of Islam," *Religion and American Culture* 12, no. 2 (2002): 167–96.

29 Quoted in Manning Marable, ed., *Dispatches from the Ebony Tower: Intellectuals Confront the African American Experience* (New York: Columbia University Press, 2000), 227.

30 Curtis, *Black Muslim Religion*, 24–31, 136–53.

31 Ibid., 109–18, 167–74.

32 Ibid., 118–27.

33 The use of the law by the Nation of Islam is covered in Sarah Barringer Gordon, *The Spirit of the Law: Religious Voices and the Constitution in Modern America* (Cambridge, MA: Harvard University Press, 2010), 96–132.

34 See the pioneering account of Kathleen M. Moore, *Al-Mughtaribun: American Law and the Transformation of Muslim Life in the United States* (Albany: State University of New York Press, 1995), 69–102.

35 Curtis, *Black Muslim Religion*, 26–27, 106–7, 141–43.

36 Ibid., 102–9.

37 Thomas M. Shapiro, *The Hidden Cost of Being African American: How Wealth Perpetuates Inequality* (New York: Oxford University Press, 2004); Melvin L. Oliver and Thomas M. Shapiro, *Black Wealth/White Wealth: A New Perspective on Racial Inequality* (New York: Routledge, 2006).

38 Angela Hanks, Danyelle Solomon, and Christian E. Weller, "Systematic Inequality: How America's Structural Racism Helped Create the Black-White Wealth Gap," Center for American Progress, February 21, 2018, www.american-progress.org.

39 Edward E. Curtis IV, "Science and Technology in Elijah Muhammad's Nation of Islam: Astrophysical Disaster, Genetic Engineering, UFOs, White Apocalypse, and Black Resurrection," *Nova Religio* 20, no. 1 (August 2016): 5–31.

40 Curtis, *Black Muslim Religion*, 86–93.

41 "Black Muslim," *New York Times*, February 28, 1975, 32.

42 Nathan Irvin Huggins, *Black Odyssey: The African-American Ordeal in Slavery* (New York: Vintage, 1990), xlviii.

CHAPTER 3. MALCOLM X AND THE ISLAMIC POLITICS OF GLOBAL BLACK LIBERATION

1 Malcolm X Diary, July 1964 (microfilm: reel 9), Malcolm X Collection: Papers, 1948–1965, Schomburg Center for Research in Black Culture, New York Public Library.

2 Gamal Abdel Nasser, *Philosophy of the Revolution* (Cairo: Dar al-Maaref, 1955), 53–54.

3 Shabazz's diaries and letters from 1964 and 1965, kept in storage by Shabazz's family and only made available to scholars and the general public in the early twenty-first century, present previously unknown data about the leader, especially about the five months that he spent in Africa and the Middle East in 1964. They record his impressions of both African and West Asian people and places, and the Muslim, African, and Arab activists, politicians, students, and others whom he met; provide information about his daily devotional prayers as a Muslim and his training as an Islamic missionary; and illustrate his constant rethinking of how Islamic religion and Pan-Africanism might produce justice and dignity for people of color around the world. For more on the history of these documents, see "Malcolm X Papers Find a Home at NYPL," *American Libraries* 34 (February 2003): 18.

4 Manning Marable, *Malcolm X: A Life of Reinvention* (New York: Viking Penguin, 2011), 12. Marable's book generated enormous controversy and several rejoinders. See, for example, "A Fiery Debate on New Malcolm X Biography: Amiri Baraka v. Michael Eric Dyson," *Huffington Post*, May 19, 2011, www.huffingtonpost.com; Herb Boyd et al., eds., *By Any Means Necessary: Malcolm X: Real, Not Reinvented* (Chicago: Third World Press, 2012); and Jared Ball and Todd Steven Burroughs, eds., *A Lie of Reinvention: Correcting Manning Marable's Malcolm X* (Baltimore: Black Classic Press, 2012). For critiques of what is sometimes called Malcolmology, or the hagiographies of Malcolm X, see Michael Eric Dyson, *Making Malcolm: The Myth and Meaning of Malcolm X* (New York: Oxford University Press, 1995), and compare "Notes on the Invention of Malcolm X" and "Malcolm X and the Failure of Afrocentrism," in Gerald Early, *The Culture of Bruising* (Hopewell, NJ: Ecco, 1994), 233–58. See also Nell Irvin Painter, "Malcolm X across the Genres," *American Historical Review* 98 (1993): 432–39. For critiques of Malcolm X biographies, compare bibliographical essays in Louis A. DeCaro Jr., *On the Side of My People: A Religious Life of Malcolm X* (New York: New York University Press, 1997), 297–300, and Marable, *Malcolm X*, 489–93. See also Robert E. Terrill, ed., *Cambridge Companion to Malcolm X* (New York: Cambridge University Press, 2010).

5   For a discussion of the Social Gospel in US history, including theologian James
    Cone's invocation of Malcolm X in this tradition, see Gary Dorrien, *Social Ethics
    in the Making: Interpreting an American Tradition* (West Sussex, UK: Wiley, 2011),
    397–98, 404, 410–11, 570. On the disputed but influential idea that African
    American religion is, in essence, a radical freedom discourse, see Gayraud S.
    Wilmore, *Black Religion and Black Radicalism: An Interpretation of the Religious
    History of African Americans*, 3rd ed. (Maryknoll, NY: Orbis, 1998). For an
    application of this idea to African American Islamic history, see Sherman Jackson,
    Islam and the Blackamerican: Looking toward the Third Resurrection (New York:
    Oxford University Press, 2005). Jackson argues that early Black Islamic move-
    ments were "God-centered holy protest against anti-black racism."

6   For histories that analyze the Nation of Islam and Malcolm X in terms of the
    larger African American engagement with Black internationalist, Afro-Asian,
    African diasporic, and Pan-African politics during the Cold War, see Sohail
    Daulatzai, *Black Star, Crescent Moon: The Muslim International and Black
    Freedom beyond America* (Minneapolis: University of Minnesota Press, 2014);
    Mary L. Dudziak, *Cold War Civil Rights: Race and the Image of American
    Democracy* (Princeton, NJ: Princeton University Press, 2000); Kevin K. Gaines,
    American Africans in Ghana: Black Expatriates and the Civil Right Era (Chapel
    Hill: University of North Carolina Press, 2006); Robin D. G. Kelley, *Freedom
    Dreams: The Black Radical Imagination* (Boston: Beacon, 2002); Brenda Gayle
    Plummer, *In Search of Power: African Americans in the Era of Decolonization,
    1956–1974* (Cambridge, MA: Harvard University Press, 2013); Brenda Gayle
    Plummer, *Rising Wind: Black Americans and U.S. Foreign Affairs, 1935–1960*
    (Chapel Hill: University of North Carolina Press, 1996); and Penny M. Von
    Eschen, *Race against Empire: Black Americans and Anticolonialism, 1937–1957*
    (Ithaca, NY: Cornell University Press, 1997). For coverage of other African
    American appropriations of Middle Eastern symbols, literary motifs, objects, and
    other cultural elements into political protest, social empowerment, economic
    activity, or cultural innovation during this era, see Robin D. G. Kelley, *Africa
    Speaks, America Answers: Modern Jazz in Revolutionary Times* (Cambridge, MA:
    Harvard University Press, 2012); Alex Lubin, *Geographies of Liberation: The
    Making of an Afro-Arab Political Imaginary* (Chapel Hill: University of North
    Carolina Press, 2014); and Melani McAlister, *Epic Encounters: Culture, Media, and
    U.S. Interests in the Middle East since 1945* (Berkeley: University of California
    Press, 2001).

7   Elijah Muhammad, *Message to the Blackman in America* (Chicago: Temple No. 2,
    1965).

8   He departed for the hajj on April 13 and returned to New York on May 21, and
    then he left again, this time for Cairo, on July 9 and did not arrive home until
    November 24. See "Chronology of the Life and Activities of Malcolm X," Malcolm

X: A Research Site, http://brothermalcolm.net/mxtimeline.html, and compare Marable, *Malcolm X*, 297–387.

9 The chapter is thus a partial response to one of Moshek Temkin's criticisms of Marable's biography in Moshek Temkin, "From Black Revolution to 'Radical Humanism': Malcolm X between Biography and International History," *Humanity* 3, no. 2 (Summer 2012), esp. 279–80. Temkin calls for an intellectual history that traces Shabazz's international connections in order to develop a more complex view of his revolutionary thought and radical humanism. For another approach to the importance of the Arab Cold War in African American Islam, see Edward E. Curtis IV, "Islamism and Its African American Muslim Critics: Black Muslims in the Era of the Arab Cold War," *American Quarterly* 59 (September 2007), 683–709, which includes coverage of Malcolm X but does not utilize the letters and diaries that are part of the Malcolm X Papers.

10 The number of full-length studies that include coverage of Shabazz's contributions to and development inside the Nation of Islam are too many to list comprehensively, but see, for example, Clayborne Carson, *Malcolm X: The FBI File* (New York: Skyhorse Publishing, 1991); DeCaro, *On the Side of My People*; Michael A. Gomez, *Black Crescent: The Experience and Legacy of African Muslims in the Americas* (New York: Oxford University Press, 2005); Bruce Perry, *Malcolm: The Life of a Man Who Changed Black America* (Barrytown, NY: Station Hill, 1991); and Richard Brent Turner, *Islam in the African American Experience*, 2nd ed. (Bloomington: Indiana University Press, 2003).

11 DeCaro, *On the Side of My People*, 123–24.

12 See Marable, *Malcolm X*.

13 Plummer, *Rising Wind*, 258.

14 Ibid., 257–66.

15 Clegg, *Original Man*, 135–36, 189.

16 His speeches from this period until his death bear the mark of these multiple influences. See *Malcolm X: By Any Means Necessary*, ed. George Breitman (New York: Pathfinder, 1970); *Black Man, Listen* (Detroit: Broadside, 1969); *The End of White World Supremacy: Four Speeches by Malcolm X*, ed. Benjamin Goodman (New York: Merlin House, 1971); *February 1965: The Final Speeches*, ed. Steve Clark (New York: Pathfinder, 1992); *The Last Year of Malcolm X*, ed. George Breitman (New York: Pathfinder, 1968), *Malcolm X on Afro-American History* (New York: Pathfinder, 1990); *Malcolm X: The Last Speeches*, ed. Bruce Perry (New York: Pathfinder, 1970); *Malcolm X: The Man and His Ideas* (New York: Merit, 1965); and *Malcolm X Talks to Young People*, 2nd ed. (New York: Pathfinder, 1969).

17 DeCaro, *On the Side of My* People, 123–24; Marable, *Malcolm X*, 131.

18 Clegg, *Original* Man, 124; DeCaro, *On the Side of My People*, 138–39; Gomez, *Black Crescent*, 350; Marable, *Malcolm X*, 165–67; Lincoln, *Black Muslims in America*, 226; Perry, *Malcolm*, 206.

19 FBI File No. 100–399321, US Department of Justice Memorandum, July 29, 1959, as reproduced in Malcolm Little HQ File 5, p. 10, in *FBI Records: The Vault*, https://vault.fbi.gov.

20 "Arabs Send Warm Greetings to 'Our Brothers' of Color in U.S.A.," *Pittsburgh Courier*, August 15, 1959, 1.

21 Plummer, *Rising Wind*, 268.

22 Emily Jane O'Dell, "X Marks the Spot: Mapping Malcolm X's Encounters with Sudan," *Journal of Africana Religions* 3, no. 1 (January 2015).

23 Malcolm X and Alex Haley, *Autobiography of Malcolm X* (New York: Ballantine Books, 1999 [1973]), 342.

24 Daulatzai, *Black Star, Crescent Moon*, 1–44.

25 Malcolm X, *End of White Supremacy*, 71.

26 This argument was laid out most forcefully in Muhammad, *Message to the Blackman in America*.

27 DeCaro, *On the Side of My People*, 201.

28 Larry Poston, *Islamic Da'wah in the West: Muslim Missionary Activity and the Dynamics of Conversion to Islam* (New York: Oxford University Press, 1992).

29 Because the Nation of Islam was by far the most publicly prominent Muslim group in the postwar United States and Malcolm X was its most popular and media-savvy spokesperson, both the organization and its national spokesman became a target of federal surveillance and counterintelligence, media scrutiny, scholarly study, and missionary competition. On media (mis)interpretations of the NOI, see Sean McCloud, *Making the American Religious Fringe: Exotics, Subversives, and Journalists, 1955–1993* (Chapel Hill: University of North Carolina Press, 2004), 55–94.

30 Letter of Malcolm X, *New York Amsterdam News*, November 24, 1962, 39; Letter from Malcolm X, *New York Times Magazine*, August 25, 1963, 2; Malcolm X, *Malcolm X: Speeches at Harvard*, ed. Archie Epps (New York: Paragon House, 1991), 118–25.

31 DeCaro, *On the Side of My People*, 201; Hans Mahnig, "Islam in Switzerland: Fragmented Accommodation in a Federal Country," in *Muslims in the West: From Sojourner to Citizens*, ed. Yvonne Y. Haddad (New York: Oxford University Press, 2001), 75–76.

32 DeCaro, *On the Side of My* People, 162; FBI file 100–399321, sec. 9, May 23, 1963, in Carson, *Malcolm X: The FBI File*, 237.

33 On Malcolm X's shifting sense of moral geography, see Grewal, *Islam Is a Foreign Country*, 107–20.

34 Haley and Malcolm X, *Autobiography of Malcolm X*, 325, 350, and 368.

35 Letter from Charles Igram to Members of the Federation of Islamic Associations in the United States and Canada, January 7, 1964, in author's possession; Marc Ferris, "To 'Achieve the Pleasure of Allah': Immigrant Muslims in New York City, 1893–1991," in *Muslim Communities in North America*, ed. Yvonne Haddad and

Jane I. Smith (Albany: State University of New York Press, 1994), 215; Bruce Perry, *Malcolm*, 261–64; DeCaro, *On the Side of My People*, 202–3.

36 Marable, *Malcolm X*, 301.

37 Yaacov Shimoni, *Political Dictionary of the Arab World* (New York: Macmillan, 1987), 105–6.

38 Islamism was not then and is not now the sole property of any one party or organization. It can take many governmental forms and express differing political goals. See further Mohammed Ayoob, *The Many Faces of Political Islam: Religion and Politics in the Muslim World* (Ann Arbor: University of Michigan Press, 2008).

39 See Ralph M. Coury, *The Making of an Egyptian Nationalist: The Early Years of Azzam Pasha, 1893–1936* (Reading, UK: Ithaca Press, 1998).

40 Abd al-Rahman Azzam, *The Eternal Message of Muhammad*, trans. Caesar E. Farah (Cambridge, UK: Islamic Texts Society, 1993), 94.

41 Haley and Malcolm X, *Autobiography*, 327.

42 The intervention of the Azzam and the Saudi government on behalf of Shabazz is recorded in several places, including Haley and Malcolm X, *Autobiography*, 325–48; DeCaro, *On the Side of My People*, 205–7; and Marable, *Malcolm X*, 308–9.

43 Fawaz A. Gerges, *The Superpowers and the Middle East: Regional and International Politics, 1955–1967* (Boulder, CO: Westview, 1984).

44 Malcolm H. Kerr, *The Arab Cold War, 1958–1964: A Study of Ideology in Politics*, 2nd ed. (London: Oxford University Press, 1965), 21–22, 53. See further Michael C. Hudson, *Arab Politics: The Search for Legitimacy* (New Haven, CT: Yale University Press, 1977); and Paul Dresch, *A History of Modern Yemen* (New York: Cambridge University Press, 2000).

45 See Reinhard Schulze, *Islamischer Internationalismus im 20. Jahrhundert: Untersuchungen zur Geschichte der Islamischen Weltliga* (Islamic Internationalism in the Twentieth Century: Studies on the History of the Muslim World League) (Leiden, 1990); Reinhard Schulze, "Institutionalization," and "Muslim World League," in *Oxford Encyclopedia of the Modern Islamic World*, ed. John L. Esposito (New York: Oxford University Press, 1995), 1:346–50 and 3:208–10.

46 Reinhold Schulze, *A Modern History of the Islamic World* (London: I. B. Tauris, 2002), 174.

47 Ibid., 152.

48 Jakob Skovgaard-Petersen, *Defining Islam for the Egyptian State: Muftis and Fatwas of the Dar al-Ifta* (Leiden: Brill, 1997), 189.

49 Schulze, *Islamischer Internationalismus*; Schulze, "Institutionalization"; Schulze, "Muslim World League"; Jacob Landau, *The Politics of Pan-Islam: Ideology and Organization* (Oxford: Oxford University Press, 1990).

50 "Appeal to African Heads of State," *Malcolm X Speaks*, 72–77.

51 "Universal Declaration of Human Rights," United Nations, www.un.org.

52 Rosemary Corbett, personal correspondence, September 13, 2018.

53 "History of New York City: United Nations Headquarters," Blogs by the TTLC, November 14, 2016, blogs.shu.edu.

54 Marable, *Malcolm X*, 342–43.

55 Ibid., 343, 351, 359, 399.

56 Marable, *Malcolm X*, 330–31; DeCaro, *On the Side of My People*, 241.

57 Most of the correspondence between Akbar Muhammad and Malik Shabazz held as part of the Malcolm X Collection occurred when both Muhammad and Shabazz were still associated with the Nation of Islam. Most of Muhammad's letters were written when he was in Cairo; the dates of the letters are September 20, 1961; November 6, 1961; November 11, 1961; April 26, 1962; February 3, 1963; March 14, 1963 (from Zanzibar); July 28, 1963; and November 9, 1964.

58 Selma Botman, *Egypt from Independence to Revolution, 1919–1952* (Syracuse, NY: Syracuse University Press, 1991), 116; Heather J. Sharkey, *American Evangelicals in Egypt: Missionary Encounters in an Age of Empire* (Princeton, NJ: Princeton University Press, 2008), 333, 334, 338, 340, and 420.

59 It is clear that Shabazz sometimes deviated from his written remarks at various points, and he was obviously talented as a debater and extemporaneous speaker. Unless otherwise stated, this article favors what is actually recorded in Shabazz's handwritten diaries since (1) they seem to be reliable historical documents, (2) they give us an unprecedented look into Shabazz's development as a thinker, and (3) reading all of the diary entries together renders a more coherent picture of Shabazz's thought.

60 Malcolm X Diary, July 1964.

61 Ibid.

62 Ibid.

63 Ibid.

64 Ibid.

65 Press Release from James Shabazz, June 6, 1964, quoted in DeCaro, *On the Side of My People*, 239. Emphasis in the original.

66 *Malcolm X Speaks*, 61–62.

67 Pace Edward E. Curtis IV, "Why Malcolm X Never Developed an Islamic Approach to Civil Rights," *Religion* 32 (2002): 227–42.

68 DeCaro, *On the Side of My People*, 33–37, 269–70.

69 For evidence of the appeal of Nasserism as a legitimately Islamic ideology, see articles such as "Socialism in Islam" and "Arab Socialism Is in the Spirit of Islamic Belief" that appeared in the Egyptian journal *Minbar al-Islam*, and John L. Esposito, *Islam and Politics*, 4th ed. (Syracuse, NY: Syracuse University Press, 1998), 134. According to Daniel Crecelius, *Minbar al-Islam* was "the single most important attempt by a group of writers to lay out the major concepts of a socialist ideology drawn from Islamic principles." Daniel Crecelius, "The Course of Secularism in Modern Egypt," in *Islam and Development*, ed. John L. Esposito (Syracuse, NY: Syracuse University Press, 1980), 234n30.

70 *Mapping Islamic Actors in Egypt*, Netherlands-Flemish Institute in Cairo/ Al-Ahram Center for Political and Strategic Studies, March 2002, 36, http:// media.leidenuniv.nl/legacy/mapping-islamic-actors---version-2.2.pdf.

71 Shabazz recorded the number of different countries represented as seventy-four, while Marable says that it was ninety-three. Marable, *Malcolm X*, 364.

72 Malcolm X Diary, August 1964 (microfilm: reel 9), Malcolm X Collection, New York Public Library.

73 Haley and Malcolm X, *Autobiography*, 357.

74 Malcolm X Diary, August 1964.

75 Ibid.

76 Ibid.

77 Schulze, *Modern History*, 173.

78 Perry, *Malcolm X*, 322; DeCaro, *On the Side of My People*, 239–41.

79 Malik El-Shabazz to Muhammad Sarur al-Sabban, November 30, 1964 (microfilm: reel 3), Malcolm X Collection, New York Public Library.

80 Ibid.

81 Malik El-Shabazz to Muhammad Taufik Oweida, November 30, 1964 (microfilm: reel 3), Malcolm X Collection, New York Public Library.

82 Malcolm X Diary, April 1964.

83 Marable, *Malcolm X*, 312.

84 Malcolm X, *February 1965: The Final Speeches*, 252–53.

85 For an orientation to the political dimensions of US religion, see, for example, Kenneth D. Wald and Allison Calhoun-Brown, *Religion and Politics in the United States*, 6th ed. (Lanham, MD: Rowman & Littlefield, 2011). The idea that the United States is at heart a secular country has been critiqued in many places, including Tracy Fessenden, *Culture and Redemption: Religion, the Secular, and American Literature* (Princeton, NJ: Princeton University Press, 2007).

86 The miracle motif is also part of modern Christianity's race relations theories. See, for example, Michael O. Emerson and Christian Smith, *Divided by Faith: Evangelical Religion and the Problem of Race in America* (New York: Oxford University Press, 2000).

87 Leila Ahmed, *A Quiet Revolution: The Veil's Resurgence from the Middle East to America* (New Haven, CT: Yale University Press, 2011), 69; John L. Esposito, "Contemporary Islam: Reform or Revolution?," in *Oxford History of Islam*, ed. John L. Esposito (New York: Oxford University Press, 1999), 667.

88 Fawaz A. Gerges, *The Far Enemy: Why Jihad Went Global* (New York: Cambridge University Press, 2005), 2–3.

89 Marable, *Malcolm X*, 329.

90 Malcolm X, *February 1965*, 104, 182.

91 Ibid., 22.

92 Edward E. Curtis IV, "African-American Islamization Reconsidered: Black History Narratives and Muslim Identity," *Journal of the American Academy of*

Religion 73, no. 3 (September 2005): 659–84, and Edward E. Curtis IV, *Black Muslim Religion in the Nation of Islam, 1960–1975* (Chapel Hill: University of North Carolina Press, 2006), 67–93.

93 Roxanne Euben, *Journeys to the Other Shore: Muslim and Western Travelers in Search of Knowledge* (Princeton, NJ: Princeton University Press, 2006), 13, 16.

94 James Clifford, *Routes: Travel and Translation in the Late Twentieth Century* (Cambridge, MA: Harvard University Press, 1997), 9–10.

95 The story of how these Islamic movements were similar to and different from other Black Power groups is one still to be told. Among the questions to be answered is how these different movements interpreted the legacy of the Nation of Islam and Malcolm X, even when they were not Islamic in nature. See, for example, the papers of Muhammad Ahmad (Max Stanford), leader of the Revolutionary Action Movement, in John H. Bracey Jr. and Sharon Harley, eds., *The Black Power Movement* (microfilm: 17 reels, LexisNexis, 2003), part 3, Papers of the Revolutionary Movement, 1962–1996. For an account that weaves the Nation of Islam into the story of Black Power, see William L. VanDeburg, *New Day in Babylon: The Black Power Movement and American Culture, 1965–1975* (Chicago: University of Chicago Press, 1992).

96 See R. H. Mukhtar Curtis, "Urban Muslims: The Formation of the Dar ul-Islam Movement," in *Muslim Communities in North America*, ed. Yvonne Y. Haddad and Jane I. Smith (Albany: State University of New York Press, 1994), 51–73; McCloud, *African American Islam*, 64–72; Dannin, *Black Pilgrimage to Islam*, 65–70; Lawrence H. Mamiya, "African-American Muslims," in *Encyclopedia of Muslim-American History*, ed. Edward E. Curtis IV (New York: Facts on File, 2010), 1:17; Khaled Fattah Griggs, "Islamic Party in North America: A Quiet Storm of Political Activism," in *Muslim Minorities in the West: Visible and Invisible*, ed. Yvonne Haddad and Jane I. Smith (Lanham, MD: Altamira, 2002), 77–106; Khalid Fattah Griggs, *Come Let Us Change This World: A Brief History of the Islamic Party of North America, 1971–1991* (Winston-Salem, NC: VisionMedia, 2007).

97 Mamiya, "African-American Muslims," 15; Dannin, *Black Pilgrimage to Islam*, 68–69.

CHAPTER 4. THE TRANSNATIONAL ETHICS OF FOUR MUSLIM AMERICAN WOMEN IN JORDAN

1 For a documentary history of this period, see Edward E. Curtis IV, *The Columbia Sourcebook of Muslims in the United States* (New York: Columbia University Press, 2008).

2 For an introduction to orientalist discourse and its role in US policies toward the Middle East, see Zachary Lockman, *Contending Visions of the Middle East: The History and Politics of Orientalism* (New York: Cambridge University Press, 2004), especially 182–267.

3 Zareena Grewal, *Islam Is a Foreign Country: American Muslims and the Global Crisis of Authority* (New York: New York University Press, 2014), 125–45.

4 Richard Brent Turner, *Islam in the African American Experience*, 2nd ed. (Bloomington: Indiana University Press, 2003), 174–238; Edward E. Curtis IV, *Islam in Black America* (Albany: State University of New York Press, 2002), 107–27.

5 Edward E. Curtis IV, *Muslims in the Military: Centuries of Service* (Bloomington: Indiana University Press, 2016), 38–42.

6 Sohail Daulatzai, *Black Star, Crescent Moon: The Muslim International and Black Freedom Beyond America* (Minneapolis: University of Minnesota Press, 2012), 159–65.

7 United Press International, "Ford and Muhammad Ali" (photograph), December 10, 1974, digitalcommons.chapman.edu.

8 Mattias Gardell, *In the Name of Elijah Muhammad: Louis Farrakhan and the Nation of Islam* (Durham, NC: Duke University Press, 1996).

9 Kambiz GhaneaBassiri, *A History of Islam in America* (New York: Cambridge University Press, 2010), 309–18.

10 John L. Esposito, *The Islamic Threat: Myth or Reality?*, 3rd ed. (New York: Oxford University Press, 1999); Fawaz Gerges, *America and Political Islam: Clash of Cultures or Clash of Interests?* (New York: Cambridge University Press, 1999); David W. Lesch, ed., *The Middle East and the United States*, 5th ed. (Boulder, CO: Westview, 2014).

11 Edward W. Said, *Covering Islam: How the Media and the Experts Determine How We See the Rest of the World*, rev. ed. (New York: Vintage, 1997).

12 Anne Norton, *On the Muslim Question* (Princeton, NJ: Princeton University Press, 2013), 3.

13 Sylvester A. Johnson, *African American Religions, 1500–2000: Colonialism, Democracy, and Freedom* (New York: Cambridge University Press, 2015), 398–99.

14 Sherene Razack, *Casting Out: The Eviction of Muslims from Western Law and Politics* (Toronto: University of Toronto Press, 2008), 1–22.

15 Ibid., 8, 10, 12.

16 Louise A. Cainkar, *Homeland Insecurity: The Arab American and Muslim American Experience after 9/11* (New York: Russell Sage Foundation, 2009).

17 George W. Bush, "Islam Is 'Peace,'" Islamic Center of Washington, DC, September 17, 2001, georgewbush-whitehouse.archives.gov.

18 Norton, *Muslim Question*, 67. For an analysis that situates Muslim American women's responses to this phenomenon within the context of their long history, see Sylvia Chan-Malik, *Being Muslim: A Cultural History of Women of Color in American Islam* (New York: New York University Press, 2018).

19 Lila Abu-Lughod, "Do Muslim Women Really Need Saving? Anthropological Reflections on Cultural Relativism and Its Others," *American Anthropologist* 104, no. 3 (September 2002): 789.

20 Cainkar, *Homeland Insecurity*.

21 Peter Gottschalk and Gabriel Greenberg, *Islamophobia and Anti-Muslim Sentiment: Picturing the Enemy*, 2nd ed. (Lanham, MD: Rowman & Littlefield, 2018).

22 Sunaina Maira, *Missing: Youth, Citizenship, and Empire after 9/11* (Durham, NC: Duke University Press, 2009), 113. See also Sally Howell and Andrew Shryock, "Cracking Down on Diaspora: Arab Detroit and America's 'War on Terror,'" *Anthropology Quarterly* 76, no. 3 (2003): 443–62.

23 Grewal, *Islam*, 256.

24 Louise Cainkar, "Learning to Be Muslim—Transnationally," *Religions* 5 (July 28, 2014): 594–622.

25 Steven Hahn, *A Nation under Our Feet: Black Political Struggles in the Rural South from Slavery to the Great Migration* (Cambridge, MA: Harvard University Press, 2005), 3.

26 Su'ad Abdul Khabeer, *Muslim Cool: Race, Religion, and Hip Hop in the United States* (New York: New York University Press, 2016).

27 Cainkar, "Learning to Be Muslim," 597.

28 Arjun Appadurai, *Modernity at Large: Cultural Dimensions of Globalization* (Minneapolis: University of Minnesota Press, 1996).

29 Sacvan Berkovitch, *The American Jeremiad* (Madison: University of Wisconsin Press, 1978).

30 Albert Hourani, *Arabic Thought in the Liberal Age, 1798–1939* (Cambridge, UK: Cambridge University Press, 1983), 128; Curtis, *Islam in Black America*, 122–23.

31 As quoted in Charles Kurzman, *The Missing Martyrs: Why There Are So Few Muslim Terrorists* (New York: Oxford University Press, 2011), 48.

32 Kurzman, *Missing Martyrs*, 49.

33 Ulf Hannerz, *Transnational Connections: Culture, People, Places* (London: Routledge, 1996).

34 Grewal, *Islam,* 7.

35 Ibid.

36 Cainkar, "Learning to Be Muslim," 617.

37 Ibid., 619.

CHAPTER 5. BLOOD SACRIFICE AND THE MYTH OF THE FALLEN MUSLIM SOLDIER IN US PRESIDENTIAL ELECTIONS AFTER 9/11

1 Jonathan Z. Smith's *HarperCollins Dictionary of Religion* insists that the fundamental constitutive element of myth is the presence of superhuman beings. But the definition of myth, much like religion itself, remains highly contested. See "Myth," in *HarperCollins Dictionary of Religion* (New York: HarperCollins, 1995), 749–51.

2 Bruce Lincoln, *Discourse and the Construction of Society: Comparative Studies of Myth, Ritual, and Classification*, 2nd ed. (New York: Oxford University Press, 2014), 23.

3 For an extensive bibliography on anti-Muslim racism, see Su'ad Abdul Khabeer, Arshad Ali, Evelyn Alsultany, Sohail Daulatzai, Lara Deeb, Carol Fadda, Zareena Grewal, Juliane Hammer, Nadine Naber, and Junaid Rana, "Islamophobia Is Racism," https://islamophobiaisracism.wordpress.com.

4 Sophia Rose Arjana, *Muslims in the Western Imagination* (New York: Oxford University Press, 2015); Thomas S. Kidd, *American Christians and Islam: Evangelical Culture and Muslims from the Colonial Period to the Age of Terrorism* (Princeton, NJ: Princeton University Press, 2013); Carl W. Ernst, ed., *Islamophobia in America: The Anatomy of Intolerance* (New York: Palgrave Macmillan, 2013); Melani McAlister, *Epic Encounters: Culture, Media, and U.S. Interests in the Middle East, 1945–2000* (Berkeley: University of California Press, 2001).

5 Lincoln, *Discourse*, 24.

6 Jonathan H. Ebel, *G.I. Messiahs: Soldiering, War, and American Civil Religion* (New Haven, CT: Yale University Press, 2015), 2.

7 Perry Miller, *Errand into the Wilderness* (Cambridge, MA: Harvard University Press, 1956).

8 Ebel, *G.I. Messiahs*, 19.

9 Ibid., 3; Edward T. Linenthal, *Changing Images of the Warrior Hero in America: A History of Popular Symbolism* (New York: E. Mellen, 1982), 120.

10 For a brief overview of US Muslim military history, see Edward E. Curtis IV, *Muslim Americans in the Military: Centuries of Service* (Bloomington: Indiana University Press, 2016).

11 One illustrative moment of this racialization in the 2008 presidential campaign was when a woman asked Republican candidate John McCain about his Democratic rival, Barack Obama, whom the woman called an Arab, which for her seemed to be synonymous with being Muslim. For more, see Junaid Rana, "The Story of Islamophobia," *Souls* 9, no. 2 (2007): 148–61; and compare Saher Selod, "Citizenship Denied: The Racialization of Muslim American Men and Women Post-9/11," *Critical Sociology* 41, no. 1 (2014): 77–95.

12 Kelly Hayes, personal correspondence, May 23, 2017.

13 "'Meet the Press' Transcript for Oct. 19, 2008," *NBC News*, www.nbcnews.com.

14 See, for example, William T. Cavanaugh, *The Myth of Religious Violence: Secular Ideology and the Roots of Modern Conflict* (New York: Oxford University Press, 2009).

15 Wilfred Owen, "Dulce et Decorum Est," *Poetry Foundation*, www.poetryfoundation.org.

16 Carolyn Marvin and David W. Ingle, "Blood Sacrifice and the Nation: Revisiting Civil Religion," *Journal of the American Academy of Religion* 64, no. 4 (1996): 774.

17 Agnieszka Soltysik Monnet, "War and National Renewal: Civil Religion and Blood Sacrifice in American Culture," *European Journal of American Studies* 7, no. 2 (2012): 8.

18 Arjun Appadurai, *Modernity at Large: Cultural Dimensions of Globalization* (Minneapolis: University of Minnesota Press, 1996); Linda Basch, Nina Glick Schiller, and Cristina Szanton Blanc, *Nations Unbound* (Amsterdam: Gordon and Breach, 1994); Ulf Hannerz, *Transnational Connections: Culture, People, Places* (London: Routledge, 1996).

19 For an introduction to a range of Islamist approaches from Islamist democracies in Indonesia and Turkey to Islamist national resistance movements in Palestine and Chechnya, see Mohammed Ayoob, *The Many Faces of Political Islam: Religion and Politics in the Muslim World* (Ann Arbor: University of Michigan Press, 2007).

20 Monnet, "War and National Renewal," 8.

21 C. Travis Webb, "'Otherwordly' States: Reimagining the Study of 'Civil' Religion," *Journal of the American Academy of Religion* 86, no. 1 (March 2018): 62–93, esp. 82–86.

22 Ebel, *G.I. Messiahs*, 9, 23.

23 Ji-Young Um, "Citizen and Terrorist, Citizen as Terrorist," *Postmodern Culture* 22, no. 3 (May 2012), doi:10.1353/pmc.2012.0009.

24 McAlister, *Epic Encounters*, 255.

25 Video with Platon in "Why Colin Powell's Emotional Obama Endorsement Is Going Viral Again," *Huffington Post*, August 5, 2016, www.huffingtonpost.com.

26 Um, "Citizen and Terrorist."

27 Shruti L. Mathur, "Blast Kills Jersey Shore GI," *South Jersey Courier Post*, August 10, 2007, as reproduced in "Kareem Rashad Sultan Khan," Arlington National Cemetery Website, www.arlingtoncemetery.net.

28 Monnet, "War and National Renewal," 10.

29 Um, "Citizen and Terrorist."

30 Curtis, *Muslim Americans in the Military*.

31 Monnet, "War and National Renewal," 3.

32 Maryann Spoto and Wayne Woolley, "Ocean GI Is State's 80th Casualty," *New Jersey Star Ledger*, August 10, 2007, https://blog.nj.com.

33 Khizr Khan, "Speech to the 2016 Democratic National Convention," July 28, 2016, https://abcnews.go.com.

34 The account above is based on Missy Ryan, "Capt. Humayun Khan, Whose Grieving Parents Have Been Criticized by Trump, Was 'an Officer's Soldier,'" *Washington Post*, August 2, 2016, www.washingtonpost.com; and Dana J. J. Pitard, "I Was Capt. Khan's Commander in Iraq," *Washington Post*, August 3, 2016, www.washingtonpost.com.

35 Monnet, "War and National Renewal," 3–4.

36 Khan, "Speech to the 2016 Democratic National Convention."

37 Transcript of "This Week," *ABC News*, July 31, 2016, https://abcnews.go.com.

38 Pitard, "I Was Capt. Khan's Commander in Iraq."

39 Ghazala Khan, "Trump Criticized My Silence. He Knows Nothing about Me," *Washington Post*, July 31, 2016, www.washingtonpost.com.

40 Charles Hurt, "Khizr Khan Was Tricked into Smearing Donald Trump," *The Hill*, July 31, 2016, http://thehill.com.

41 For context, see further Maryam Khalid, "Feminist Perspectives on Militarism and War," in *The Oxford Handbook of Transnational Feminist Movements*, ed. Rawidda Baksh and Wendy Harcourts (New York: Oxford University Press, 2015), 632–50.

42 "U.S. Presidential Visits to Domestic Mosques," White House Historical Association, accessed February 14, 2019, www.whitehousehistory.org.

43 Louise A. Cainkar, *Homeland Insecurity: The Arab American and Muslim American Experience after 9/11* (New York: Russell Sage, 2009); Trevor Aaronson, *The Terror Factory: Inside the FBI's Manufactured War on Terrorism* (New York: Ig Publishing, 2014); Alia Malek, *Patriot Acts: Narratives of Post-9/11 Injustice* (San Francisco: McSweeney's Books, 2011); Human Rights Watch, *Illusions of Justice: Human Rights Abuses in US Terrorism Prosecutions* (New York: Human Rights Watch and Columbia University, Human Rights Institute, 2014), www.law.columbia.edu.

44 Council of American-Islamic Relations, "CAIR Releases Results of Presidential Election Exit Poll," November 22, 2016, www.cair.com.

45 Ismat Sarah Mangla, "Hillary Clinton Has an Unfortunate Way of Talking about American Muslims," *Quartz*, October 20, 2016, https://qz.com.

46 "No Regrets, Trump Vows as Clinton Ad Targets His Criticism of Muslim-American Family," *Chicago Tribune*, October 21, 2016, www.chicagotribune.com.

47 Monnet, "War and National Renewal," 10–13.

48 German Lopez, "Polls Show Many—Even Most—Trump Supporters Deeply Hostile to Muslims and Nonwhites," *Vox*, September 12, 2016, www.vox.com.

49 Aziz Rana, "Against National Security Citizenship," *Boston Review*, February 7, 2018, http://bostonreview.net.

50 Zareena Grewal, *Islam Is a Foreign Country: American Muslims and the Global Crisis of Authority* (New York: New York University Press, 2013), 341.

51 Sylvester A. Johnson, *African American Religions, 1500–2000: Colonialism, Democracy, and Freedom* (New York: Cambridge University Press, 2015), 394. See also Junaid Rana, *Terrifying Muslims: Race and Labor in the South Asian Diaspora* (Durham, NC: Duke University Press, 2011).

52 Johnson, *African American Religions*, 404.

CONCLUSION

1 Anne Norton, *On the Muslim Question* (Princeton, NJ: Princeton University Press, 2013), 1–3.

2 Abdolmohammad Kazemipur, *The Muslim Question in Canada: A Story of Segmented Integration* (Vancouver: University of British Columbia Press, 2014), 1–7.

3 Norton, *Muslim Question*, 3.

4 Sunaina Marr Maira, *Missing: Youth, Citizenship, and Empire after 9/11* (Durham, NC: Duke University Press), 276.

5 Ibid., 201.

6 Ibid., 250.

7 Alan Feuer, "Linda Sarsour Is a Brooklyn Homegirl in a Hijab," *New York Times*, August 7, 2015, www.nytimes.com.

8 "The Muslim Community Rises with Ferguson: From Palestine to Ferguson," *Ummah Wide*, October 17, 2014, https://ummahwide.com.

9 "Mayor De Blasio and Chancellor Fariña Designate Eid Al-Fitr and Eid Al-Adha Official School Holidays," NYC Department of Education, March 4, 2015, www.schools.nyc.gov.

10 Michael M. Grynbaum and Sharon Otterman, "New York City Adds 2 Muslim Holy Days to Public School Calendar," *New York Times*, March 4, 2015, www.nytimes.com.

11 "Champions of Change: Linda Sarsour," White House, accessed February 14, 2019, https://obamawhitehouse.archives.gov.

12 Azi Paybarah, "A Brooklyn Democrat Who Called Obama 'Terrible' on Civil Rights Will Be Honored by the White House," *Politico*, December 14, 2011, www.politico.com.

13 Deepa Iyer and Linda Sarsour, "Obama Wants to 'Counter Violent Extremism': He Should Look beyond Muslims," *Guardian*, February 17, 2015, www.theguardian.com.

14 Kristin McLaren, "Muslim Innovations in American Exceptionalist Rhetoric: Linda Sarsour's American Jeremiad," *Journal of Religion and Popular Culture* 29, no. 2 (Summer 2017): 154.

15 "Linda Sarsour Speech at Washington Square Park: Bernie Sanders Rally," April 14, 2016, YouTube video, 4:02, posted by Leland T. Snyder, May 1, 2016, www.youtube.com/watch?v=H_WuS6xtaos.

16 "MPower Change," MPower Change, accessed February 14, 2019, http://mpower-change.org.

17 Leah Fessler, "Women's March Leader Linda Sarsour: Stop Telling Me to Go Back to My Country. I'm from Brooklyn," *Quartz*, February 6, 2018, https://work.qz.com.

18 Linda Sarsour, "Organizer Linda Sarsour's Speech at Women's March on Washington," YouTube video, 4:59, posted by Democracy Now, January 23, 2017, www.youtube.com/watch?v=EUWc4le60Ak.

19 "What Is BDS?," BDS, accessed February 14, 2019, https://bdsmovement.net.

20 It is hard to find academic studies that do not take an explicit political position on BDS. For a number of informed essays on the movement from its academic advocates, see Ashley Dawson and Bill V. Mullen, eds., *Against Apartheid: The Case for Boycotting Israeli Universities* (Chicago: Haymarket Books, 2015).

21 See, for example, Jason Lemon, "This Muslim Activist Got a Rape Threat and Pointed Out the Irony on Twitter," *StepFeed*, July 12, 2017, https://stepfeed.com.

22 Eli Rosenberg, "A Muslim-American Activist's Speech Raises Ire Even Before It's Delivered," *New York Times*, May 26, 2017, www.nytimes.com.

23 "Linda Sarsour Gives CUNY Commencement Speech: 'Commit to Never Being Bystanders,'" *Time*, June 2, 2017, www.time.com.

24 Emma-Kate Symons, "Agenda for Women's March Has Been Hijacked by Organizers Bent on Highlighting Women's Difference," *Women in the World*, January 19, 2017, https://womenintheworld.com.

25 Bari Weiss, "When Progressives Embrace Hate," *New York Times*, August 1, 2017, www.nytimes.com.

26 Gaby del Valle, "Why Do Liberals Love to Hate Linda Sarsour?," *The Outline*, August 3, 2017, https://theoutline.com.

27 "'I Will Not Be Bullied, Intimidated, Threatened over My Unshakeable Support for Palestinian Liberation'—Linda Sarsour," *Mondoweiss*, August 4, 2017, https://mondoweiss.net.

28 McLaren, "Muslim Innovations," 152, 154, 155.

29 Ibid., 158.

30 "Linda Sarsour Arrested at Paul Ryan's Office," *AlJazeera*, March 6, 2018, www.aljazaeera.com.

31 Clayborne Carson, *Malcolm X: The FBI File* (New York: Carroll and Graf, 1991), 79–80; Malcolm X, *February 1965: The Final Speeches*, ed. Steve Clark (New York: Pathfinder, 1990), 11–23.

32 See Sohail Daulatzai and Junaid Rana, eds., *With Stones in Our Hands: Writings on Muslims, Racism, and Empire* (Minneapolis: University of Minnesota Press, 2018).

33 Linda Sarsour, Facebook post, January 3, 2019, accessed March 11, 2019, www.facebook.com.

34 Mike DeBonis and Robert Costa, "McCarthy Pressures Democrats to Rebuke Two Muslim Lawmakers over Alleged Anti-Semitism," *Washington Post*, February 8, 2019, www.washingtonpost.com; Sam Brodey, "Who's Afraid of Ilhan Omar? Saudi Arabia for One," *MinnPost*, December 18, 2018, www.minnpost.com.

INDEX

Abboud, Deedra, 20
Abdullah, Mustafa, 146–47
Abdul-Rauf, Muhammad, 43
Abdul-Samad, Ako, 21
Abedin, Huma, 21
Abu Ghraib prison, 32
Abu-Salha, Razan, 27–28
Abu-Salha, Yusor, 27–28
activism: Black Lives Matter, 146–48, 153;
    boycotting for, 149; dissent as, 145–46;
    economics of, 49–50; *The Eternal
    Message of Muhammad* (Azzam) for,
    70; for immigrant Muslims, 138; with
    nonviolence, 52–53; politics and, 15–16,
    151–52; for UAR, 74
Adams, John, 4
Afghanistan, 13–14, 96, 140, 152
Africa, 78–80, 91, 136. *See also specific
    countries*
African Americans: American Dream for,
    52; Arabs and, 62–64; Black capital-
    ism, 8, 34–35, 49, 51; Black Power
    groups for, 177n95; *Christianity, Islam,
    and the Negro Race*, 36; Christianity
    for, 58; civil liberties for, 36; econom-
    ics for, 168n20; generational poverty
    for, 51; global black liberation, 56–60,
    71–72, 81–82, 85–86; Islam for, 83–84;
    leadership for, 25–26, 34–35, 77–78;
    liberalism for, 53–54, 59, 74–75, 82–83;
    military for, 38–39; Muslims and, 7,
    144–45; NAACP for, 37; national-
    ism for, 2, 41; politics of, 14; racism
    against, 76, 93; slavery of, 21; socialism

for, 53–54; UN and, 70–71; in US, 1,
    61, 75–76; white supremacy for, 49;
    women, 44–46. *See also* minorities
Ahmad, Muhammad, 177n95
Ahmadiyya movement, 36
Ali, Dusé Mohamed, 36
Ali, Muhammad, 38, 42, 47–48, 54, 87,
    90–91
Ali, Saqib, 21
al-Qaeda, 30, 98
America. *See* United States
American Civil Liberties Union, 146–47
American Jeremiad (Bercovitch), 153–54
El-Amin, T. D., 21
El-Amin, Yaphett, 20–21
anti-Muslim activity, 26–27. *See also*
    Islamophobia
Antoniou, Platon, 129, 134
Arabs: African Americans and, 62–64;
    Cold War for, 8, 66–71, 172n9; Islam
    and, 43–44; leadership for, 39; Mus-
    lims and, 75–77, 114–18, 146, 180n11;
    NNAAC for, 147; racism against,
    24–25, 101–2, 109–10; in US, 22;
    women, 110–14. *See also* United Arab
    Republic
Arendt, Hannah, 94
Asha, Rafik, 62
al-Assad, Bashar, 136
assimilation, 1–2, 11, 18, 26–33, 94–95,
    165n46
Autobiography of Malcolm X, 77
Azzam, Abd al-Rahman, 63, 66–68, 70
Azzam, Omar, 67–68

ABOUT THE AUTHOR

Edward Curtis is co-founder and co-editor of the *Journal of Africana Religions*. He is the author or editor of multiple books on Islam and Muslims in the United States and in the African Diaspora, including *The Practice of Islam in America: An Introduction.*